ANTHROPOLOGY AND THE OLD TESTAMENT

J. W. ROGERSON

JOHN KNOX PRESS
ATLANTA

Library of Congress Cataloging in Publication Data

Rogerson, John William.
    Anthropology and the Old Testament.
    Bibliography: p. 121
    Includes index.
    1. Man (Theology)—Biblical teaching. I. Title.
BS1199.M2R63   1979   233   78-14234
ISBN 0-8042-0083-1

© Copyright Basil Blackwell 1978
First published in Great Britain in 1978
Published in the United States of America in 1979 by
John Knox Press
Atlanta, Georgia

Printed in Great Britain

Contents

Acknowledgements

The suggestion that I should write this book came from Professor G. W. Anderson. I wish to record my deep gratitude to him for the suggestion, and also for his criticisms of two drafts. The final version has also profited from the criticisms of my colleague Canon Douglas Jones, and of Mr. Douglas Davies, a Durham graduate in social anthropology and in theology, and now a lecturer in the Department of Theology, University of Nottingham.

The initial research on the Old Testament material was done in Erlangen in the summer of 1972. This was made possible by a Visiting Fellowship awarded by the British Academy, and by the generosity and friendship of Professor D. Dr. Georg Fohrer, Professor of Old Testament in the University of Erlangen-Nürnberg. Subsequent research was carried out in the summer of 1974 in the University Library, Tübingen, to whose staff I should also like to extend my thanks.

Durham, March 1978   J. W. Rogerson

I

Anthropology and the Old Testament

The Old Testament is a collection of books which can be studied from several angles. In addition to being Holy Scripture for Jews and Christians, it is the major source for our knowledge of the ancient Hebrew language, ancient Hebrew and Jewish history, and ancient Hebrew law and society. However, the information which the Old Testament provides on these topics is often only partial, and thus it has long been the case that the Old Testament has been studied in the light of information gained from other disciplines. The meanings of some Hebrew words have been established with the help of other related Semitic languages; historical narratives have been understood within the wider setting of ancient Near Eastern history; legal sections have been seen to have affinities with the laws of the ancient Near East. Furthermore, these seemingly non-theological matters have been regarded as important to theologians, and it has been acknowledged that the theologian needs all the information he can get about the language, history, law, and society of the people of the Old Testament, if he is to do justice to his attempt to understand the divine self-disclosure to which witness is borne in its pages. Accordingly, the scholarly equipment required by the student of the Old Testament has become formidable. Depending on his special interests, he will have studied some or all of the following disciplines: theology, philosophy, archaeology, Semitic and Classical languages, egyptology, linguistics.

One discipline, however, has been omitted from the list of disciplines likely to be studied by Old Testament specialists—anthropology (which provisionally we shall understand as the study of man's social organization, customs, folklore and beliefs, together with theoretical generalizations or assumptions about these things). It has been omitted deliberately, because it has been rare for an Old Testament scholar to be trained as an anthropologist (an exception was the late S. H. Hooke). Yet for at least two hundred years, Old Testament scholars have made judgements about the Old Testament which rested on anthropological assumptions, and they possibly have at least as many areas of common concern with anthropologists as with egyptologists or assyriologists. Indeed, the matter is complicated by the fact that egyptologists and assyriologists also make assumptions which are essentially anthropological assumptions, and the Old Testament scholar may be in danger of applying to the Old Testament, anthropological conclusions reached in these other fields by specialists who may know no more about anthropology than he does.

In defence of the Old Testament scholar, and the other specialists mentioned, it must be said that after the long apprenticeship that has to be served in their respective fields, they may well find that the prospect of tackling yet another complex discipline like anthropology is daunting. However, the task has to be carried out, and the present book will be worth while if it indicates to the reader that the relation between Old Testament study and anthropology presents a problem, and if it indicates the resources for solving that problem. It must be stressed that this book is not the work of a professional anthropologist, but of an Old Testament student who has done a good deal of anthropological reading.

This opening chapter will review the history of anthropology, with particular reference to the Old Testament. It is hoped thereby to define 'anthropology' more carefully, and to demonstrate its importance for Old Testament study.

The second half of the eighteenth century roughly marks the beginning of the modern critical study of the Old Testament. It also marks the first attempts by Old Testament scholars to use anthropology in a serious methodological way. Already long before the eighteenth century, travellers, missionaries, and consular officials to the East, and especially to Egypt, Syria-Palestine, and Arabia, had noted customs and other aspects of the way of life of the inhabitants of those lands, which seemed to shed light on passages in the Old Testament. At the beginning of the second half of the eighteenth century, the Göttingen orientalist and Old Testament scholar J. G. Michaelis, sought to put such activities on a proper scientific footing. He pressed publicly for the sponsoring of an expedition of trained observers to the Near East, observers who would know the relevant languages of the area, and who would work to a properly planned scheme of observation and research. Michaelis did not despise the work already done by travellers and missionaries, but as he pointed out, the accounts of such observers tended to cover the same sort of ground, whereas they must have seen countless things which, had they been trained observers, they would have known to be of great interest to Old Testament scholars.[1]

As a result of Michaelis's suggestions, a scholarly expedition to the East was organized, under the patronage of King Frederick V of Denmark. It consisted of an orientalist, a botanist, a doctor, a painter, and a surveyor, and it set out for the East in 1761. In the following year, Michaelis published one hundred questions which he had addressed to its members. This is not the place to record the adventures of the expedition, of which four members died before its planned research had been completed. The survivor, the surveyor Carsten Niebuhr, performed a most remarkable task in completing much of the work of the expedition single-handed, and his accounts of his journeys, which were published from 1772 onwards, had great influence on subsequent Old Testament study, as will be indicated.[2]

The majority of Michaelis's questions to the expedition were not themselves particularly anthropological. Mostly, they dealt with the identification of plants or illnesses or animals mentioned in the Old Testament, or they asked geographical questions, for example the tidal state of the Red Sea at the point where the Israelites were presumed to have crossed it at the time of the Exodus. But if Michaelis's questions were not particularly anthropological, the theoretical assumption of the whole enterprise was. This assumption was that the desert had somehow preserved for

[1] J. D. Michaelis, *Fragen an eine Gesellschaft Gelehrter Männer die auf Befehl Ihro Majestät des Königes von Dännemark nach Arabien reisen*, Frankfurt, 1762, preface (the pages of which are not numbered).

[2] The fullest account of the expedition in English is that of Thorkild Hansen, *Arabia Felix*, London, 1964, trans. from *Det Lykkelige Arabien*, Copenhagen, 1962. See also the relevant parts of D. G. Hogarth, *The Penetration of Arabia*, London, 1905.

nearly four thousand years the sort of life lived by the Israelites
in the time of Abraham, Isaac, and Jacob, and that it was possible
to reconstruct something of that life by observing contemporary
dwellers of the desert, especially the Bedouin. The point of such
reconstruction would be to enable obscure parts of the Old
Testament to be better understood. This anthropological assumption could not, of course, be shown to be true. It was based only
on the apparent similarity between customs and practices described in the Old Testament, and customs and practices found
in the contemporary Near East; but it was an assumption to be
made many times subsequently by Old Testament scholars. In
the following chapter, it will be more closely examined; for the
moment we note it as an assumption of Old Testament study
which has been operative for at least two hundred years.

The comparison of contemporary Arabian Bedouin with the
Hebrew patriarchs was not an unreasonable exercise. At least the
two groups lived in roughly the same geographical region, and the
comparison did seem to be supported by apparent correspondences
in their customs and practices. However, the eighteenth century
also provides evidence that Old Testament scholars were prepared
to utilize knowledge about so-called primitives of the day to
illumine parts of the Old Testament. For example, Michaelis's
interests were not confined to Arabia. He read about primitives as
far afield as North America, Greenland, and Mongolia, and in
1763 published a paper which in some ways anticipated the work
of the British Old Testament scholars of over one hundred years
later, especially that of W. Robertson Smith.[3] In this paper,
Michaelis sought to explain the origin of the institution known as
levirate marriage in the Old Testament.

Levirate marriage in ancient Israelite society is not perhaps as
well understood by modern scholars as they would wish, but the
institution would appear to be a way of preserving the rights of
inheritance of a man who has died childless, and of providing a
status for his widow.[4] In such a case, it is the duty of the deceased

---

[3] Michaelis, ' Ius Leviratus Israeliticum Explicatum ' in *Commenta-*
tiones Societatis Regiae Scientiarum Goettingensi, 1763. Also *Mosaisches*
Recht, 6 vols., 1770–5, Göttingen, para. 98.

[4] Cp. Deut. 25:5–10, Ruth 3:13, 4:1–10 and the commentaries thereon.
Cp. also Gen. 38, and *Notes and Queries on Anthropology*, London, 1951[6],
pp. 117–18.

husband's eldest brother to take the widow to wife, so as to produce a child who would be the heir of his dead 'father'. Michaelis explained the origin of this institution by reference to an account of life in Mongolia.[5] He suggested that there had been a time in ancient Arabia, as apparently in Mongolia, when there had been a shortage of women. The shortage had produced a type of social organization in which a group of brothers shared one wife. Then, one man had become powerful or rich enough to possess a wife of his own. On the death of such an individual, the wife would pass to the deceased's brothers. Later still, this only happened when the deceased died childless. From here, it was only a short step to the institution of levirate marriage as described in the Old Testament.

Michaelis was not in this case making the assumption commonly made in the eighteenth and nineteenth centuries, that all races had passed through identical stages of development, and that therefore what could be observed of contemporary less-developed societies must once also have held good in ancient societies. His position was rather that both in Mongolia and ancient Arabia, a similar situation had existed in which women were in short supply because they were taken off as slaves by superior neighbouring peoples. However, this position assumed that given similar social situations, societies would react to them in similar ways. What is most interesting about Michaelis's argument is that it anticipates an approach that was to be dominant in the nineteenth century, whereby what seem to the modern writer to be *logical* connections between phenomena are turned into *historical* connections. Michaelis had no actual historical evidence about the origin of levirate marriage in ancient Israel; but what seemed to him to be a plausible *logical* connection between levirate marriage, and polyandry as practised in Mongolia, was presented as the *actual historical* origin and development of the Old Testament institution.

Michaelis's work was only part of a considerable amount of research by Old Testament scholars in the second half of the eighteenth century, devoted to providing material from the East

[5] Michaelis was dependent for his knowledge of Mongolia on the writings of the Frenchman J. B. du Halde, and his *Description géographique, historique, chronologique et physique de l'Empire de la Chine et de la Tartarie Chinoise*, Paris, 1735.

that would contribute to the understanding of the Old Testament. In 1789, E. F. K. Rosenmüller published a German edition of descriptions of the East by the French government official L. d'Arvieux. D'Arvieux (1635–1702) had spent some twelve years in the Palestine area from 1653–65. The merits of his book, published posthumously in 1717, had apparently first been recognized by Michaelis, who in question 58 of his questions to the Arabia expedition had asked for its accuracy to be checked. Carsten Niebuhr had confirmed its accuracy in glowing terms,[6] and accordingly, Rosenmüller was able to recommend his new translation and edition of the book as a work 'which accurately portrays the customs of a people that has preserved the pastoral, nomadic way of life of its ancestors, Abraham, Isaac, and Jacob in a pure form, and free from foreign customs.'[7] Not long after Rosenmüller's publication, the rationalist theologian H. E. G. Paulus issued the first of his seven volumes which, between 1792 and 1803 made available to German readers selections of the most important accounts of travellers in the East.[8] Paulus gave pride of place to the account of a journey from Aleppo to Jerusalem made in 1697 by a British chaplain, the Reverend H. Maundrel, together with the same man's journey two years later to the Euphrates and Mesopotamia. Other excerpts included accounts of journeys by a M. Peter Belon at the end of the sixteenth century, and accounts furnished by Jesuit and Protestant missionaries of the seventeenth century. It is particularly striking that, at the end of the eighteenth century, evidence that originated from two hundred years earlier in some cases, was being assembled, so that it could be passed on to influence Old Testament scholarship in the nineteenth century. Yet given the assumption that the desert had preserved intact the life of the biblical patriarchs over the centuries, there could be no objection to evidence on the score of its antiquity, provided that one accepted the integrity of the observer. In England, similar material was published, and very often re-published in Germany. The writings of the arabist Richard (later Bishop) Pococke were

---

[6] Carsten Niebuhr, *Beschreibung von Arabien*, Copenhagen, 1772, p. 30.

[7] E. F. K. Rosenmüller, *Die Sitten der Beduinen-Araber. Aus dem Französischen des Ritters Arvieux*, Leipzig, 1789, p. ix. (Translation by the present writer.)

[8] H. E. G. Paulus, *Sammlung der merkwürdigsten Reisen in den Orient*, Jena, 1792–1803.

influential,[9] as was Harmer's collection of comments on passages of Scripture, which were gleaned from travel accounts, and materials such as the *Gesta Dei per Francos* (the accounts of the Crusaders in Syria/Palestine).[10]

No less important was the work of the Göttingen classicist C. G. Heyne. Heyne used accounts about the life and customs of 'savages' of his day in order to explain the origin of crude elements in Greek myths.[11] Briefly, his theory was that primitive (and thus also ancient) man personified the forces of nature around him, or conceptualized natural occurrences in terms of supernatural beings. Heyne's theory of primitive mentality was introduced into Old Testament study by another Göttingen scholar J. G. Eichhorn, who used it as the basis of the first attempt in biblical scholarship to demythologize the Bible with the help of a theory of primitive mentality.[12] Eichhorn's application of the theory to Genesis 2–3, for example, assumed that the narrative was basically historically correct. There had been a pair of human beings in a garden, and they had eaten the fruit of a tree which was poisonous. The poison had affected their physical constitution, making them aware for the first time of physical passions, and thereby beginning the process of human reproduction. A storm in the evening had terrified them, and in confusion, they had fled from the garden. Such were the historical facts. The present form of the narrative,

[9] R. Pococke, *Description of the East and some other Countries*, London, 1743–5; German translation, Erlangen, 1754.

[10] Thomas Harmer, *Observations on Various Passages of Scripture grounded on circumstances incidentally mentioned in Books of Voyages into the East*, London, 1764, 1776² (Vols. 1 and 2), 1787 (Vols. 3 and 4). German translation of Vols. 1 and 2 by J. E. Faber, Hamburg, 1772. See the generous review by Michaelis in *Orientalische und Exegetische Bibliothek*, Frankfort, V (1773), pp. 210–12. Michaelis also reviewed the 2nd edition of the German edition of Pococke (Erlangen, 1771–3) in Vol. VIII (1775), pp. 108–15 of the *Orientalische und Exegetische Bibliothek*.

[11] C. G. Heyne, *Opuscula Academica*, Göttingen, 1779, I, pp. 184–206, III, pp. 1–30. Note the title of the essay in Vol. III, 'Vita anti-quissimorum hominum, Graeciae maxime, ex ferorum et barbarorum populorum comparatione illustrata.' Heyne seems to have relied heavily on J. Carver's *Travels through the interior parts of North America*, London, 1778.

[12] J. G. Eichhorn in *Repertorium für Biblische und Morgenländische Litteratur*, IV, 1779.

which included a talking serpent and God holding conversation with the couple, derived from the way in which alone the earliest humans could conceptualize and understand the world. Of course, serpents do not talk, but the earliest humans thought that the serpent they saw (which perhaps ate the fruit and was not harmed) did. Again, God did not actually converse with them, but when they heard the noise of the storm, they thought that God was speaking, and condemning them for their disobedience. Other supernatural elements in the story could be similarly explained.

Seen in the context of the sort of exegesis of Genesis that was current at the end of the eighteenth century, this interpretation is not nearly so crude as it appears to the modern reader. In its day, it represented an attempt to maintain the integrity of the biblical text understood in the light of a theory about the way earliest humans conceptualized the world about them. However, we are more concerned with the anthropological assumptions involved. Apart from the identification of contemporary primitives with earliest man, Heyne's theory assumed the correctness of the anthropological evidence on which he depended for his information about the thought processes of primitives; but it is to be doubted whether the information available to his informants was really first-hand, or whether it was based on a knowledge of the language of the primitives concerned. The fact that Eichhorn's exposition of Genesis 2–3 seems astonishingly crude to the modern reader, should not make him think that the underlying anthropological assumptions are to blame. Exactly the same anthropological assumptions have been made time and time again since Heyne and Eichhorn by Old Testament scholars, but because the resultant biblical interpretations have accorded with the outlook of their various times, no one has thought to question the underlying assumptions.[13]

Examples of the use in Old Testament study of anthropological assumptions could be multiplied at this point without difficulty. However, because such examples will be described throughout the book, further comment here would be superfluous. Elsewhere in the book it will be shown how some of these eighteenth-century

[13] Numerous examples of the interpretation of the Old Testament in the light of theories about myth and primitive mentality will be found in my book *Myth in Old Testament Interpretation*, Berlin, 1974.

assumptions continued their influence even into the present century.

At the beginning of the chapter, anthropology was defined provisionally as the study of man's social organization, customs, folklore and beliefs, together with theoretical generalizations or assumptions about these things. It is now necessary to consider the scope and aims of anthropology more carefully, and to do this by paying attention to the history of the discipline. First of all, it should be noted that there are differences in the way anthropology is organized and understood, as between Britain and America. Also, European terminology seems to differ from that of Britain and America. The easiest difference to appreciate is that the German word *Anthropologie* does not entirely correspond to the British 'anthropology.' The German word is more commonly used to denote theories or speculation about the nature and being of man, and although in theological works in English it is possible to find 'anthropology' used to denote the nature and destiny of man, it would be fair to say that the modern user of English would not regard this as the *primary* sense of 'anthropology'.[14] The German word *Ethnologie* conveys more of what is primarily meant in English by 'anthropology' and the nearest French equivalent is probably *sociologie*.

In both Britain and America today, there is agreement that anthropology should be divided into at least two main branches, of which one is called physical anthropology. This has been defined as the study of 'man as a biological animal; his origins and sub-human relations; early man; and the development of modern man, with stress upon racial and other differentiation.'[15] Apart from this, the agreement on terminology is less than unanimous. American usage, as described by Keesing, contrasts with physical anthropology, cultural anthropology (a term not used in Britain as far as I am aware) which in turn is sub-divided into prehistoric archaeology, linguistic anthropology, and ethnology. The last term

[14] It is something of a surprise to the present writer that H. W. Wolff's *Anthropologie des Alten Testaments*, Munich, 1973, which is mainly an attempt to reconstruct the Old Testament view of the nature of man, and his place in the world, should have been translated as *Anthropology of the Old Testament*, London, 1974.

[15] F. Keesing, *Cultural Anthropology*, New York, 1958, p. 4.

is further sub-divided into ethnography (the study of a specific culture), ethnology (a study of likenesses and differences among cultures) and social anthropology ('the development of scientific generalizations about a culture, or about culture, society and personality in a more universal sense').[16] Against this, British usage tends to contrast social anthropology directly with physical anthropology, and one definition of the former is the study of 'social behaviour, generally in institutionalized forms, such as the family, kinship systems, political organization, legal procedures, religious cults and the like, and the relations between such institutions'.[17] In Britain it would be recognized, of course, that prehistoric archaeology and linguistics are important for anthropology, the former perhaps more important for physical anthropology; but it would not, I think, be British practice to regard these disciplines as part of anthropology.[18]

In the present book, the main preoccupation will be with social anthropology as understood in Britain, and the definition quoted above will serve as a reasonable guide. On occasion, however, the discussion will be widened so as to include matters of concern to cultural anthropology. Always, we shall be concerned to note the influence on Old Testament study of theoretical assumptions from these fields. The difference between British and American terminology is probably the result of the history of anthropological studies, and whereas British social anthropology has become interested above all in society (i.e. the study of relationships and institutions within particular societies) American study has concentrated on culture (i.e. the comparison of customs and beliefs found in many societies). Indeed, the emergence of social anthropology as a discipline in Britain can be said to be the story of the making of the distinction between culture and society, and the concentration upon the latter.[19]

[16] Op. cit., p. 5.

[17] E. E. Evans-Pritchard, *Social Anthropology*, London, 1951, p. 5.

[18] However, a new interest in linguistics by British social anthropologists should be noted. See E. Ardener (ed.), *Social Anthropology and Language*, London, 1971; Hilary Henson, *British Social Anthropologists and Language*, Oxford, 1974.

[19] For an American account of the history of anthropology see F. W. Voget, 'The History of Cultural Anthropology' in J. J. Honigmann (ed.), *Handbook of Social and Cultural Anthropology*, Chicago, 1973, pp. 1–88. Voget divides his study into four main periods: General Social Science

In his book *Social Anthropology*, E. E. Evans-Pritchard divided the history of anthropology into three periods. The first was roughly from the eighteenth century to the middle of the nineteenth century; the second from the mid-nineteenth century to the early twentieth century, and the third beginning roughly fifty years ago. According to Evans-Pritchard, the majority of the important writers of the first period were philosophers such as Hume and Adam Smith who 'for the most part . . . used facts to illustrate or corroborate theories reached by speculation.'[20] These writers did not, apparently, know a great deal about the primitive societies of their day, but what they did know was enough to convince them of the importance of these societies for theories about the nature and development of social institutions. The main theoretical assumption in this first period was that human nature was sufficiently constant to allow one to presume that 'our forefathers must have lived the same kind of life as the Redskins of America and other primitive peoples when they lived in similar conditions and at a similar level of culture.'[21] Evans-Pritchard further notes that 'we have already in the speculations of these eighteenth-century writers all the ingredients of anthropological theory in the following century, and even at the present day.'[22]

During this first period, direct anthropological influence on Old Testament study is hard to trace, if only because there was no discipline of anthropology as such, but rather, philosophers making anthropological-type inferences. On the other hand, the writings of British philosophers were known in Germany at this time, and especially in Göttingen where Michaelis and Heyne worked.[23] Also, the brief description at the beginning of this chapter of the anthropological assumptions underlying Old Testament work in

---

(c. 1725–1840), Evolutionism (c. 1840–90), Structuralism and the Rise of Social and Cultural Determinism (c. 1890–1940) and developments since 1940. It is to be noted that by 'structuralism,' Voget does not mean the structuralism described in chapter 6 of the present book. Rather, he refers to the work of Durkheim and Mauss in France and of Radcliffe-Brown in Britain. Voget's first two periods seem to correspond roughly with Evans-Pritchard's first two periods (see above).

[20] Evans-Pritchard, *Social Anthropology*, p. 27.   [21] Ibid., p. 24.
[22] Ibid., p. 25.
[23] C. Hartlich and W. Sachs, *Der Ursprung des Mythosbegriffes in der modernen Bibelwissenschaft*, Tübingen, 1952, pp. 169–71, discuss the possible influence of Hume on Heyne.

this period will indicate how much the scholars concerned shared the assumptions outlined by Evans-Pritchard. Perhaps it would be less true to say of Old Testament scholars of this period what Evans-Pritchard says about the philosophers, that they 'used facts to illustrate or corroborate theories reached by speculation.'[24] In the nature of the case, they were trying to understand difficult passages in the Old Testament, and they did not have their minds already made up as to what the solutions might be.

The second period described by Evans-Pritchard, that from the mid-nineteenth century to the beginning of the present century, was probably the most important period for anthropological influence on the Old Testament. It was characterized by men of great erudition, and an amazing capacity for work; men such as Sir James Frazer, who corresponded with observers all over the world and who collected vast quantities of material about the life and customs of primitives.[25] In this period, there was an interest in the material for its own sake, rather than a desire to use it to prove theories reached by speculation. But the material itself raised difficult questions for the men of this period, and they were especially exercised in their minds by the apparent similarities of belief and custom to be found among differing peoples throughout the world. Thus they sought to frame theories that would account for these similarities, and in Evans-Pritchard's words, 'it was they who first brought together the information about primitive peoples from a wide range of miscellaneous writings and presented it in systematic form, thereby laying the foundation of social anthropology.'[26]

Their main assumptions were evolutionistic, and they used a comparative method for the purposes of historical reconstruction. In the absence of actual historical evidence for the origin and development of beliefs and customs, they nevertheless tried to build up an historical picture of how human societies, social institutions and religious beliefs had originated and grown, and they based their reconstructions on a comparison of beliefs and customs from many parts of the world. They assumed that all races had passed through identical stages of social, mental, and religious

[24] See note 20.
[25] Cp. R. A. Downie, *Frazer and the Golden Bough*, London, 1970, p. 111.
[26] Evans-Pritchard, *Social Anthropology*, p. 28.

development, and that the forebears of civilized peoples had once lived, thought, and believed like contemporary primitives. They sought to show how science had developed from magic, how marriage as understood in Western society had evolved from promiscuity; how, beginning with nomadism, some societies had developed into industrialized countries. The fact that sometimes the reconstructions were totally contradictory did not seem to cast doubt on the assumptions and methods used. For example, in books published in the same year, 1861, Sir Henry Maine argued that the original and universal form of family life was the patri-archal family, with dominance of the father, and inheritance in the male line, while J. J. Bachofen maintained that the original and universal form of the family was the matriarchal family with inheritance in the female line.[27]

The attraction of such methods and writings for Old Testament scholars will not be difficult to see. It has already been pointed out that although the Old Testament is the major source for our knowledge about ancient Hebrew society, the evidence that it provides is often incomplete. However, if all peoples had indeed passed through identical stages of social and mental development, and if anthropologists could reconstruct these stages, then Old Testament study could expect to get from anthropology a good deal of illumination for the more sketchy parts of ancient Israelite social and religious history. This can be illustrated by a typical and important example.

One of the books referred to by Evans-Pritchard as being an early theoretical classic from this period is the book by the French-man Fustel de Coulanges entitled *La cité antique*.[28] The book was first published in 1864. It was not concerned primarily with primitive societies, but it was nevertheless an attempt to describe the development of social life from its most primitive origins to the foundation of the ancient city. Most of the evidence was from ancient Greece and Rome, but, where necessary, reference was made to ancient Indian literature, and to the life of primitives in Africa and North America.[29] The principal thesis was that the

---

[27] Evans-Pritchard, *Social Anthropology*, p. 29.
[28] Op. cit., p. 27. Reference is here made to Fustel de Coulanges, *La cité antique. Étude sur le culte, le droit, les institutions de la Grèce et de Rome*, Paris, 1866².
[29] Fustel de Coulanges, pp. 34–5.

patriarchal family was the most primitive form of social life. Yet the family was formed not 'by nature,' but by religion. Belief in the survival of the soul was strong among primitives, and at the death of a person his family would commemorate him at the shrine to be found in the house, and at his tomb. Thus, there would exist an extended family of brothers and their families, bound together by the worship of a common ancestor. Later, with the passing generations, although the extended family might itself sub-divide into large families each with its more recent ancestors, the worship of the more ancient common ancestor would continue, until the whole group of families became a tribe, bound together by common worship. Later still, a group of tribes would unite to form a larger social unit, the city. Naturally, this is a somewhat over-simplified account of the first three parts of Fustel de Coulanges's book. However, two points that have been described were taken over into German Old Testament scholarship of the period. They were the points, first, that it was religious belief which generated and held together the earliest forms of social organization, and second, that this religious belief was in the first instance ancestor worship.

From the year 1881, the influential German scholar Bernhard Stade published his history of the ancient Israelites.[30] This was a large-scale work, which treated not only the political history of ancient Israel, but also its social and legal history. Stade took a sceptical view of the information in the Old Testament about the origins of ancient Israel. According to him, the Old Testament genealogies did not give accurate information about the origins of the Hebrews; rather, they reflected what writers at varying periods of Israel's history conceived to be the contemporary political relationships between Israel and her neighbours. Traditions about ancestors of the past were often fictitious, invented by writers who, because they thought that a tribe or a people ought to have a great ancestor, supplied the traditions where they were lacking.

Having chosen to ignore the admittedly difficult and fragmentary evidence contained in the Old Testament about ancient Israel's origins, Stade turned to Fustel de Coulanges for a theory with which he could describe the history of Israel's earliest social institutions and religion. With very little modification of de

[30] B. Stade, *Geschichte des Volkes Israel*, Berlin, 1881.

Coulanges's theories about the origin and growth of tribes and cities,[31] Stade argued that in the ancient Semitic and thus Israelite family, the religion was ancestor worship, and that this worship both generated and maintained the solidarity of the social institutions. Stade also followed de Coulanges by asserting that these two facts explained the power of the father over his family, and the laws of inheritance through the male line. Religion was thus also the force behind law.[32]

The influence of Stade's history in Germany was considerable, and he was followed, among others, by Wellhausen. In the next chapter, more examples will be given of the dependence of important Old Testament writings on anthropological assumptions and reconstructions of this second period, and it should be noted that, in some cases, such influence lasted into the present century. For the moment, the generalization can be made that, in numerous ways, Old Testament scholars of the second period utilized the histories of social institutions and religion made by anthropologists. Further, the Old Testament itself was sometimes used as evidence, as a link in the chain of witnesses in the historical reconstruction.

Commenting in retrospect on this second period, Evans-Pritchard points out that 'very little indeed was then known about primitive societies and what were taken for facts were very often not facts at all but superficial observations or prejudiced opinion.' He adds that 'their (the writers of this period) use of the comparative method for the purpose of historical reconstructions led them into unjustifiable, and totally unverifiable, conclusions.'[33] This will be illustrated when the third period of anthropology is considered. Before we turn to that, however, it must be emphasized that Evans-Pritchard's criticisms of the anthropologists of the second period are not criticisms made disdainfully from a lofty and superior standpoint. The important contributions made by the

[31] Stade admitted his indebtedness to Fustel de Coulanges on p. 390, note 1. However, he criticized de Coulanges for not allowing the possibility that when two families unconnected by blood united together under a covenant, the ancestor of one of the families would be reckoned as the common ancestor, and the ancestor of the other family would be reckoned as a more recent ancestor of both groups.

[32] Stade, pp. 390 ff. De Coulanges explicitly refers to the Old Testament on p. 76.

[33] Evans-Pritchard, *Social Anthropology*, pp. 36–7.

Victorian anthropologists are gratefully recognized as the necessary
prelude to the third period in the history of anthropology. Similarly, the Old Testament scholars of this period must not be
dismissed simply because they took over the assumptions of their
day, even if such assumptions are now seen to be highly questionable. What should worry the Old Testament student is the fact
that today there seems to be insufficient awareness in the Old
Testament field of the extent to which the assumptions made in
the second period are no longer tenable. The continuing use of
such assumptions in Old Testament study should be a real matter
for concern.

The third period in the history of anthropology can be characterized by two words—fieldwork and functionalism. The founders
of this third period in Britain were A. R. Radcliffe-Brown and
B. Malinowski, and they pioneered that approach to the study of
primitive societies which involved learning the language and living
among the people being studied (fieldwork), and describing the
society concerned in terms of the contribution of each particular
aspect of its life to the maintenance of the society as a whole
(functionalism). This new approach revealed the defects of some
of the work of the second period of anthropology. For example, the
information collected about primitives during this earlier period
was often misleading. The observers with whom men such as
Frazer had corresponded had been sincere, but they had not lived
among the people whom they described. Often they lived separately
in mission or administrative compounds, and their visits inter-
rupted the normal flow of life of the 'natives.' They had had no
training in anthropological theory, and they often judged what
they saw from pre-conceived religious or 'civilized' standpoints.
Fieldwork discovered that many primitive peoples were by no
means primitive in some aspects of their lives, for example, in
their kinship systems, and they were found to be more logical in
their thought than had been supposed, if their beliefs and values
were interpreted functionally, that is, in the light of their contribution to the total life of the society.

Fieldwork and functionalism emphasized the distinction between
culture and society, as defined earlier in this chapter. The anthropologists of the second period had interested themselves primarily
in culture, that is, in beliefs, customs, and usages, and these things
had been plucked out of their social contexts, and had been made

the subject of sweeping comparisons and generalizations. Field-work and functionalism, on the other hand, concerned themselves not with broad generalizations, but with the detailed study of individual societies, and especially with the religious, political, legal, and kinship networks of relationships which make up individual societies. Further, this concentration in depth brought about a deliberate self-limitation on the part of social anthropology (as we must now call it) in its claims to knowledge. Social anthropology saw itself as essentially descriptive, its task being to describe the structures of societies where such evidence was available. It did not see its task as the reconstruction of the origin and history of human institutions and religious beliefs. It was of the opinion that the evidence required for such reconstructions was largely lacking, and it criticized the anthropologists of the second period for plucking customs and beliefs from their social contexts in making such reconstructions.

In view of all this, it will come as no surprise that Evans-Pritchard has defined social anthropology in the following way:

> Social anthropology studies ... social behaviour, generally in institutionalized forms such as the family, kinship systems, political organization, legal procedure, religious cults and the like and the relations between such institutions; and it studies them either in contemporaneous societies or *in historical societies of the kind to make such studies feasible.*[34]

This quotation, and especially the part which is italicized, should be carefully noted by students of the Old Testament. The stress on fieldwork and functionalism, which has led in turn to the emergence of social anthropology as defined above, has also led to a method of study which may have mainly negative implications for the Old Testament. Not only does social anthropology doubt the possibility of the sort of reconstructions of man's religious, mental, and social past that were once eagerly seized upon by Old Testament specialists and are still not without influence among them, it also raises the question whether in fact the Old Testament contains adequate information for ancient Israelite society to be reconstructed or understood with any degree of certainty. We are reminded that second-period anthropology was utilized in Old

[34] Op. cit., p. 5 (italics mine).

Testament study precisely because it was believed to be able to fill in gaps in the evidence provided by the Old Testament.

However, the negative implications of third period anthropology for the Old Testament might in fact be gains. In the first place, it will do no harm to Old Testament study to have to recognize more clearly the limits of what it can know about ancient Israelite society. Secondly, the corrective to many of the theories of second-period anthropology which come from the third period, should lead to a reappraisal of Old Testament standpoints that are dependent on discredited second-period anthropological assumptions. Also, there is at least one area in which Old Testament study has been positively influenced by functionalism. I refer to the interpretation of myth in myth and ritual terms, and to the way in which Malinowski's essay *Myth in Primitive Psychology*[35] has helped Old Testament interpreters to understand myths not just as written texts, but as a dramatic part of the life of the people, making a contribution to their social stability and self-understanding.

However, the title of the present book deliberately begins with the word 'anthropology,' because while much that follows will be indebted to British social anthropology, it will not be forgotten that there are other facets of anthropology. Further, it must be noted that British social anthropology is constantly submitting itself to criticism, in the hope of gaining new insights. For example, although the third period of the history of anthropology has been summed up by the words fieldwork and functionalism, these have their limitations, as experts in the field recognize. It is freely acknowledged that fieldwork is often done under very difficult conditions, and that workers often spend far less time in the field than they would like. Also, societies do change, and a description of a primitive society based on fieldwork done in the nineteen fifties, while valid for that time, will not be valid for all time.

In the 1950s and 1960s, functionalism was increasingly seen to be an approach, the usefulness of which in social anthropology was limited. Because it described the way in which the various parts of a social system function in relation to the whole society, it had given the impression that primitive societies were always in a

[35] B. Malinowski, *Myth in Primitive Psychology*, 1926, reprinted in *Magic, Science and Religion*, New York (Doubleday Anchor Books), 1954, pp. 93–148.

balanced state of equilibrium, and that they did not change.[36] But of course they do change, and where proper historical evidence is available, the study of such social change is an important part of anthropology and sociology. Curiously enough, the recognition of the limits of functionalism is also an implicit criticism of the one aspect in which Old Testament study has been indebted to third-period anthropology, namely the 'myth and ritual' understanding of myth. For in Old Testament study, it has often been assumed that where we find myths, they are performed in order to achieve some sort of social or cosmic status quo. It is rarely asked whether such myths (if indeed it is the case that they are connected with rituals—a point which cannot often be proved) represent a present and living attempt to shape and control cosmic forces, or whether their performance is no more than a custom, whose purpose is not clearly understood.

Much has been made in this chapter of the distinction between society and culture; but even here we must note that this useful distinction becomes dangerous if pressed too far. In fact, culture and society are merely two abstractions, concepts which are employed in order to understand the reality, which is the life of a group of people in a particular place. The concepts are in fact complementary rather than contradictory, and the relations between them are complex. This fact will serve as a reminder that although British anthropology has tended to concentrate on descriptions of particular societies, other aspects of anthropology, especially in America, have not fought shy of wider questions of comparison between differing cultures. Also, the development in recent years of structural anthropology is another attempt to break away from over-concentration on individual societies, and to seek the possibilities of cross-cultural comparison. Structural anthropology, especially as found in the writings of C. Lévi-Strauss, has sought to interpret social data, especially kinship and myth, as situational responses deriving from the structure of the human

---

[36] For criticisms of functionalism see E. E. Evans-Pritchard, *Essays in Social Anthropology*, London, 1962, Ch. 3; E. R. Leach, *Political Systems of Highland Burma*, London, 1964², pp. x ff.; J. Rex, *Key Problems of Sociological Theory*, London, 1961, Ch. 4. For a defence of the continuing usefulness of functionalism see M. Gluckman, 'The Utility of the Equilibrium Model in the Study of Social Change,' *American Anthropologist*, 70, 1968.

mind in its perception and thinking.[37] All this should be reassuring to the British Old Testament scholar if he thinks that anthropology as practised in his own country has, in recent years, become so specialized and descriptive that it can have almost no value for the Old Testament. At the same time, we see that even social anthropology is by no means marking time in its theoretical self-understanding and discoveries.

This chapter has tried to indicate something of the involvement of Old Testament study in anthropology, and something of the development of the latter as a discipline. Whatever happens in the future, one thing is here to stay, and that is the recognition that assertions about primitives can only be made on the basis of information derived from informants with knowledge of the relevant languages, and close contact with the people concerned. In this respect, the Old Testament specialist can be proud that two of his forerunners were pioneers in this field. The initiative of J. D. Michaelis in the despatch of a scientific expedition to the East has already been mentioned. However, nothing in detail has been said about the real pioneer in fieldwork, the survivor of the expedition to Arabia, Carsten Niebuhr. When his four professional colleagues died, it might easily have been concluded that the least able of the expedition had survived to complete its work. However, this was far from being the case. Two of Niebuhr's colleagues were professors, and they spent much time exercising a personal rivalry as well as a superiority over the non-professorial members of the expedition. They were disdainful of the 'natives' and wanted to live and eat in the East in a manner commensurate with their professorial status in the West. It was precisely because Niebuhr was a man of humble origins that he became most fitted to complete the expedition's work. He had begun to study Arabic under Michaelis in Göttingen, and he gained sufficient knowledge of Arabic dialects, and gained sufficient sympathy with informers to be able to elicit valuable information.

In the preface to one of his accounts of the expedition,[38]

---

[37] What is stated in this sentence is discussed more fully in chapter 6, below.

[38] Carsten Niebuhr, *Beschreibung von Arabien*. Niebuhr's other accounts were contained in *Reisebeschreibung nach Arabien und anderen umliegenden Ländern*, Vols. 1 and 2, Copenhagen, 1774–8, Vol. 3, Hamburg, 1837. An English translation of Vols. 1 and 2 of the *Reisebeschreibung*, by R. Heron,

Niebuhr stressed that the tragic loss of life should not deter subsequent expeditions. Death had occurred because some of his colleagues had been reluctant to adopt the local diet and way of life; they had wanted to live in Western fashion in the East. Niebuhr further stressed the need not only to know the language and to win the confidence of informers, but to listen to them without any preconceived criticism drawn from the listener's own religious or cultural background. It is to be regretted that while Niebuhr's writings were widely read in the nineteenth century by Old Testament students, the methods of scholarship which his accounts implied, were little heeded.

was published in 1792 and an edited version of Niebuhr's accounts was reissued in 1973 under the title *Entdeckungen im Orient. Reise nach Arabien und anderen Ländern 1761–1767*, Tübingen and Basle.

2

Survivals, Evolution and Diffusion

We shall now begin to look more closely at particular aspects of the use of anthropology in Old Testament study. Our first task will be to outline the doctrine of survivals, and its importance.[1]

If one takes a literal view of the opening chapters of Genesis, that is, if one accepts that these chapters give a true historical and social account of the original family from which the whole human race has descended, it is necessary to come to terms with certain anthropological facts. These are, first, that according to the Genesis narrative, man was created at a relatively high level of culture. Adam is from the first an agriculturalist (Gen. 2:15) and seems to have missed the food gathering and hunting stages which are usually held to have preceded the agricultural stage. Further, in Gen. 4:2, we find that one of Adam's children has already domesticated sheep, and later in the chapter (4:22) we are given the name of the inventor 'of every cutting instrument of brass and iron.' On the basis of this evidence, Adam and his family must have been well on in Neolithic or New Stone Age culture, and perhaps even a lot further on than this. As against the biblical evidence thus literally interpreted, studies from at least the eighteenth century began to reveal the existence of peoples whose level of culture was considerably lower than that of Adam. For example, the Australian aborigines had barely reached the level of Old Stone Age culture. Faced with the need to reconcile a literal

[1] See, above all, Margaret Hodgen, *The Doctrine of Survivals. A Chapter in the History of Scientific Method in the Study of Man*, London, 1935. Hodgen is followed by Mary Douglas, *Purity and Danger*, London, 1966, pp. 11 ff. For a graphic account by a folklorist see R. M. Dorson, *The British Folklorists*, London, 1968, pp. 193 ff. and *passim*.

reading of Genesis with such newly-discovered facts, theologians of the eighteenth and nineteenth centuries agreed that while man had been created at the level of New Stone Age culture, there had been a subsequent *degeneration* in the case of contemporary peoples who were found to be at a level lower than that. Theologically, this degeneration was evidence for the continual need of man for divine grace; where this grace was rejected, man sank into savagery.[2]

Degeneration was in the eighteenth and nineteenth centuries the standard theological argument against those optimists who believed that human nature inevitably progressed to higher achievements. In the nineteenth century, the theory of degeneration was taken up by no less a person than Archbishop Whately,[3] and it was partly against Whately that E. B. Tylor developed the doctrine of survivals in order to prove the theory of developmentalism once for all.[4] A survival has been compared with the mute letters to be found in some words. For example, the 'k' in the word knight is functionless in speech, but it remains as evidence of an earlier period of English when it indeed had a function. As applied to cultural data, the doctrine of survivals drew attention to the presence of functionless crude or superstitious elements of belief or custom to be found in civilized societies, usually among the peasantry of such societies. These beliefs or customs were held to be the fossilized remains, so to speak, of a time when the *whole* society had lived at the cruder level of culture suggested by these survivals. Further, if similar beliefs and customs could be found in a widespread form among contemporary primitive peoples, then the argument became even stronger. Thus, by comparing survivals found among civilized peoples with customs and beliefs found among primitives, two theories could be maintained.

[2] In a recent book, *Who was Adam?*, Exeter, 1969, E. K. Victor Pearce has used anthropology in order to support a literal interpretation of Genesis. He accepts that Adam must have been New Stone Age man, but takes the two accounts of creation in Gen. 1 and 2 as evidence for two creative acts on the part of God, the first at a lower level of culture than the second. The problem of relating Adam to primitives with much lower levels of culture is thereby avoided. However, this is a method of interpreting Genesis which is unlikely to convince many specialists.

[3] R. Whately, *On the Origin of Civilization*, London, 1855.

[4] E. B. Tylor, *Primitive Culture: Researches into the Development of Mythology, Philosophy, Religion, Art and Custom*, London, 1871.

The first was that human history was the story of progress, not degeneration. The second was that in reaching their present civilized state, civilized societies had once passed through the lower stages of culture still to be found among primitive and less civilized peoples. The stages of culture, from the lowest to the highest could be reconstructed by a comparison of beliefs and customs from all over the world.

If we wish to place the doctrine of survivals in the context of the description of the history of anthropology contained in the opening chapter, we can say that it was a method which supported the attempts of second-period anthropology to reconstruct the history of beliefs and customs by means of the comparative method. The evidence used came from the pre-fieldwork period of study, and the evidence used was largely plucked from its social context. The doctrine of survivals therefore stands under the condemnation passed on the second period of anthropology by the third period. However, as we shall now see, it exercised its influence on the Old Testament scholars of the nineteenth century, who had accepted the historical-critical method of scholarship.

In 1885, William Robertson Smith published his book *Kinship and Marriage in Early Arabia*.[5] His aim was to demonstrate that the thesis of his friend J. F. McLennan about the origin and development of the ancient family was true for ancient Semitic society, including the earliest ancestors of the Hebrews. Briefly, McLennan's theory was that, in the earliest forms of society, social units were bound together by common blood into groups, each one of which identified itself with a totem animal or similar object. Within the group, inheritance was within the female line. There had been, however, a custom of killing female children, which led first to a shortage of women, and then to the development of polyandry (i.e. the possession by several men of one wife).[6] But in its turn, polyandry had eventually led to the more widespread and familiar dominance of the male line over the female line.[7] It is not the purpose of the present book either to describe how McLennan sought to demonstrate this thesis, nor to give a detailed

[5] W. Robertson Smith, *Kinship and Marriage in Early Arabia*, London, 1885, 1907². References are to the second edition.

[6] It is on the matter of polyandry that Michaelis anticipated McLennan and Robertson Smith so remarkably.

[7] J. F. McLennan, *Primitive Marriage*, Edinburgh, 1865.

account of how Robertson Smith argued that the thesis was applicable to the most ancient Semites. In what follows, the important point will be the way in which the doctrine of survivals was used by Robertson Smith in his argument.

There are, in the Old Testament, a number of passages about kinship and marriage which seem odd, when it is considered that society as portrayed in the Old Testament is dominated by the patriarchal family. For example, in Gen. 2:24 the words:

> Therefore shall a man leave his father and his mother and shall cleave unto his wife: and they shall be one flesh.

could be understood as saying that when a man marries, he goes to live with his wife's family. Again, in Gen. 29 Jacob, on marrying Leah and Rachel, lives with his wives and his father-in-law, and does not set up an independent home until he escapes from, and is pursued by, his father-in-law. Such passages were regarded by Robertson Smith as survivals (he preferred the term 'relics')[8] from a time when, in ancient Semitic society, descent was in the female line, and the husband was adopted into his wife's kin.

It was indeed possible to build up quite a list of survivals which seemed to point in the same direction. In Gen. 34, the Shechemites had to be circumcised before they could be considered fit to become husbands for Israelite women; i.e. the presumption was that they would have to be adopted into Israel, the people to which their prospective wives belonged. In Gen. 48:5, the sons born in Egypt to Joseph by his Egyptian wife Asenath (Gen. 41:50–2) were adopted into Israel, again the assumption being that they were originally reckoned to belong to their mother's people. According to Judges 15, Samson's Philistine wife did not come to live with him, but stayed with her own people, where Samson visited her. Survivals in the Old Testament also seemed to point to the other part of McLennan's thesis which Robertson Smith wished to demonstrate for the ancient Semites, namely, that the earliest social units identified themselves with totem animals or objects. Thus the names Rachel and Leah could mean 'ewe' and 'bovine antelope' respectively; the Calebites (Heb. *keleḇ*, dog) who lived in south Judah bore the name of a dog tribe, and the name

[8] *Kinship and Marriage*, p. 207.

of the sons of Hamor who lived in Shechem (Gen. 34) really meant 'sons of the he-ass' (Heb. *ḥamor* (he-)ass).[9]

The use of survivals to demonstrate that the ancient Semites had once been totemistic in their social organization also influenced Robertson Smith's understanding of sacrifice. In *The Religion of the Semites*[10] it was argued that at the stage of totemic social organization, when a totemic group ate the totem object after which it was named, communion was established with the totem god. Robertson Smith thus believed that underlying all Semitic sacrifice, including that of the Old Testament, was the notion that its purpose was to establish communion with the deity. This was especially true of those Old Testament sacrifices in which the worshippers ate part of the sacrificial flesh.

The influence of Robertson Smith's theories based on the doctrine of survivals was wide in Old Testament scholarship, and no doubt the theoretical bases of the theories were often not understood by those who employed them. In Germany, for example, the theses that the social organization of the most ancient ancestors of the Hebrews was matriarchal and matrilineal were solemnly repeated, with the usual proof texts, by Nowack in 1894,[11] Volz in 1914[12] and Benzinger in 1927.[13] At least by Benzinger's time, it should have become apparent that few anthropologists now believed in an original universal matriarchate. The theories about communion sacrifice found their way into those most influential of works, the Hebrew lexicons. Thus the lexicon of Brown, Driver and Briggs had the following entry under *zebaḥ*: 'the common and most ancient sacrifice, whose essential rite was eating the flesh of the victim at a feast in which the god of the clan

---

[9] Op. cit., pp. 253 ff. Totemism is defined in *Notes and Queries on Anthropology*, p. 192, as 'a form of social organization and magico-religious practice, of which the central feature is the association of certain groups within a tribe with certain classes of animate or inanimate things...'

[10] W. Robertson Smith, *Lectures on the Religion of the Semites*, London, 1889, 1894[2], 1927[3], especially lecture 8. It must be stressed that Robertson Smith's account of totemism should not be accepted uncritically. For a discussion of some of the problems, see C. Lévi-Strauss, *Totemism*, London, 1962, pp. 1–14.

[11] W. Nowack, *Lehrbuch der Hebräischen Archäologie*, Freiburg and Leipzig, 1894, pp. 153 ff.

[12] P. Volz, *Die Biblischen Altertümer*, Stuttgart, 1914, pp. 333 ff.

[13] I. Benzinger, *Hebräische Archäologie*, Leipzig, 1927[3], pp. 113 ff.

shared by receiving the blood and fat pieces';[14] while as late as 1958 the lexicon of Koehler and Baumgartner could say: 'sacrifice of communion = sacrifice of slaughtered sheep, goat, cattle the eating of whose flesh creates communion between the god in whose worship the sacrifice is slaughtered and the partners of the sacrifice and communion between the partners themselves.'[15]

The use of the doctrine of survivals also had an effect on the way in which Arabic material was used in relation to the Old Testament. It was noted in the previous chapter that it had long been the custom of Old Testament scholars to use the material about life in Arabia collected by travellers, missionaries, and government officials. Scholars such as Robertson Smith were no exception.[16] However, they were aware of the dangers of doing this uncritically, and they tried to put their work on an objective footing by seeking information about pre-Islamic Arabian religion. Robertson Smith in Britain, and J. Wellhausen in Germany, searched the pre-Islamic Arabic literature for survivals of primitive Semitic religion.[17]

What Robertson Smith and Wellhausen were doing on the basis of literature was reinforced in the field by an American, Samuel Ives Curtiss, who visited Palestine and Syria in the years 1898–1902. Curtiss believed that it was possible to find survivals of primitive Semitic religion in present-day (i.e. around 1900) Syria and Palestine, although he was careful to apply criteria to his work. There were three main criteria. To be primitive, a religious belief or custom should first, not be found in Christianity or Islam, second, be discovered in areas where either Christianity or Islam normally held sway, and third, correspond with what scholars such as Robertson Smith and Wellhausen had discovered from their literary work. Curtiss's account of his researches, entitled *Primitive Semitic Religion Today*[18] supported Robertson Smith's

---

[14] F. Brown, S. R. Driver, C. A. Briggs, *A Hebrew and English Lexicon of the Old Testament*, Oxford, 1907, p. 257.

[15] L. Koehler, W. Baumgartner, *Lexicon in veteris testamenti libros*, Leiden, 1958, p. 249.

[16] See, for example, *The Religion of the Semites* (3rd ed.), pp. 279, 335.

[17] J. Wellhausen, *Reste Arabischen Heidentums*, Berlin, 1887. Robertson Smith had, of course, travelled widely. See J. S. Black and G. W. Chrystal (eds.), *Lectures and Essays*, Edinburgh, 1912, Pt. V, Ch. 2, 'A Journey in the Hejaz.'

[18] S. I. Curtiss, *Primitive Semitic Religion Today*, Chicago, 1902.

Ca

theories in numerous ways. However, he did not agree with
Robertson Smith's view of sacrifice. He confessed that in 1898–9
he had been inclined to accept the communion sacrifice as the
most primitive form of sacrifice, but as time went on, field observations convinced him that more basic to ancient Semitic sacrifice
was the notion of the giving of a life for a life, by the shedding of
the blood of the sacrificial victim.[19] Otherwise, Curtiss found
abundant evidence for belief in spirits associated with high places,
sanctuaries, stones, trees, and wells, and this evidence, as we shall
see later, became important for those who used the doctrine of
survivals to argue that the history of Israelite religion was the
story of a gradual ascent to monotheism, via animism and polytheism. Curtiss's book was translated immediately into German,[20]
the edition being commended to German readers by W. W.
Baudissin. Baudissin's introduction was not entirely uncritical;
for example, he pointed out that because a belief or custom was
not Moslem or Christian it was not therefore necessarily primitive
Semitic. But as to the method of using survivals in order to discover ancient forms of belief, Baudissin had not the slightest
reservations. After all, had not the brothers Grimm shown how
much primitive German heathenism was to be found in Christian
Germany of the nineteenth century ?[21] It will come as no surprise
to readers to be told that Curtiss's book had great influence among
Old Testament scholars who wished to interpret the history of
Israelite religion in a developmentalist way.

We now move to a consideration of the criticisms that were
levelled against the doctrine of survivals by a rival anthropological
theory of the day, namely, diffusionism. Faced with the fact that
similar customs and beliefs are to be found scattered all over the
world, two major ways of accounting for these facts have been
advanced. The first, which we have been describing, supposes
that all races have passed through similar stages of technological
and cultural development, and uses the doctrine of survivals to
support this supposition. Indeed, it is the persistence of similar
beliefs and customs all over the world which lends plausibility to
the view. It is not so easy, however, to explain how this worked in
detail. If it is asked, for example, if the assumption is that all

---

[19] Op. cit., Ch. 24.
[20] *Ursemitische Religion im Volksleben des heutigen Orients*, Leipzig, 1903.
[21] Baudissin in the introduction to *Ursemitische Religion*, p. vi.

peoples have independently made the discoveries and inventions appropriate to each stage of the development, the position looks less plausible. For it is obvious that peoples have contact with each other, that new discoveries can be passed on from one people to another, and that new forms of belief and custom are imposed upon defeated peoples by their victors. It is a short step from acknowledging these facts, to the other major way of accounting for the existence throughout the world of similar beliefs, customs and practices, namely, that such things result from diffusion from one or more centres of civilization. At the present time, a popular ally of the diffusionist view would be the Norwegian, Thor Heyerdal, whose epic voyages on the balsa raft *Kon Tiki*, and the papyrus boats *Ra I* and *II* have shown that it is *possible* that similarities of culture in countries separated by vast expanses of ocean are the result of migrations across the oceans concerned.

From roughly the beginning of the 1870s, the publication of newly-discovered cuneiform texts from Mesopotamia began to shed light on the great civilizations of ancient Assyria and Babylonia. In 1872, George Smith announced his discovery of a Babylonian flood narrative similar to that found in Genesis, and not long after, Babylonian parallels to the biblical creation narrative were claimed to have been discovered. These, and similar discoveries, resulted in the rise in Germany of the so-called pan-Babylonian school, a group of scholars who looked above all to the Babylonian material as providing the context in which the Old Testament should be interpreted. The school also claimed that Babylon was the source of much of the world's culture, which had spread from Babylon by diffusion. It also advocated an astral-mythological view of ancient texts, arguing that many epics and even historical texts had originated from or had been shaped by astral observations or descriptions of the workings of nature.[22]

Nowadays, there is a tendency to write off the pan-Babylonians as a rather curious episode in the history of Old Testament and ancient Near Eastern study, and to some extent this is justifiable. The preoccupation of the school with astral myths was a gross exaggeration of an element of truth; the attempt of some of its members to derive even the Passion Narrative of the New Testament from the Epic of Gilgamesh was little short of incredible.

[22] See H.-J. Kraus, *Geschichte der historisch-kritischen Erforschung des Alten Testaments*, Neukirchen-Vluyn, 1969², pp. 305 ff.

However, one should not be totally blind to the merits of the pan-Babylonians; and their opposition to the doctrine of survivals and the developmentalist position which it supported needs to be considered.

The whole matter can perhaps be put in better perspective if it is recalled that Robertson Smith and Wellhausen were criticized in their day for concentrating on Arabic material in their researches, whereas they ignored the much more ancient Babylonian material. This charge against Wellhausen was made, for example, by Gunkel,[23] and James Muilenburg, in his prolegomenon to a new edition of *The Religion of the Semites* recalls that it was also made against Robertson Smith.[24] However, to be fair to Robertson Smith and Wellhausen, and those who followed them, it was not that they 'ignored' the new discoveries. On the contrary, for them, the new discoveries were irrelevant. They might indeed be *ancient*, but they were certainly not *primitive*. The ancient Babylonian civilization was syncretistic; it was built on Sumerian (i.e. non-Semitic) foundations, and it had been contaminated by many non-Semitic influences. The Arabic sources, whether literary, or those investigated by Curtiss, might be much later than the Babylonian texts, but they were 'purer', and therefore a better source for reconstructing primitive Semitic religion. We see, then, that the clash between the developmentalists and the diffusionists was an important methodological clash.

The view of the diffusionists was probably most effectively put by Hugo Winckler, in a small book published in 1906, and intended as a counterblast to a book by Karl Marti on the history of Israelite religion.[25] In his book, Marti had presented a developmentalist view. He had followed Robertson Smith, Wellhausen, the accounts of travellers in the East, and especially Curtiss. A main assumption was that the religion of Islam in present-day Arabia was merely a top-coating of varnish over the primitive folk-religion of the area. The scholars whom Marti followed had discovered an astonishing number of ancient religious practices

[23] H. Gunkel, *Reden und Aufsätze*, Göttingen, 1913, p. 27.
[24] J. Muilenburg in W. R. Smith, *Lectures on the Religion of the Semites*, New York, 1969³, pp. 12, 22 of the Prolegomenon.
[25] H. Winckler, *Religionsgeschichtler und Geschichtlicher Orient*, Leipzig, 1906; K. Marti, *Die Religion des Alten Testaments unter den Religionen des vorderen Orients*, Tübingen, 1906.

living on in the East today, which could be used in the reconstruction of the history of Hebrew religion. Marti divided this
history into four main periods: the religion of a nomadic or
Bedouin people; the agricultural religion of a people newly settled;
the religion of the prophets; the religion of the law. The doctrine
of survivals was used, for example, to prove the reconstruction of
the first period. Traces of nomadism were found in Gen. 4:23–4,
and the Rechabites (Jer. 35:1–11), a sect which refused to live in
houses or to drink wine, were said to keep alive the nomadic
ideal.

Against Marti and his authorities, Winckler attacked first of all
the view of the ancient Near East which the whole position en-
tailed. Islam was not a varnish spread over the primitive folk-
religion of the Arab world. Islam had itself arisen out of that
'folk religion' and as a protest against it. The same was true of the
religion of the Old Testament, where the traditions about the
patriarchs reflected a similar protest movement. If one asked more
closely on what the folk religion was based, it was certainly not
based on the religion of primitive man, but was rather something
which had grown out of the culture which had once spread all over
the ancient Near East from ancient Babylonian civilization. In
fact, the religion to be found today in the Near East was a *degeneration* from this ancient Babylonian pattern, and in no way a source
for reconstructing primitive Semitic religion. On specific points
raised by Marti, Winckler advanced alternative suggestions. Gen.
4:23–4 was a piece of poetry reflecting only the views of the time
of its composition, and certainly not a survival of nomadism. The
Rechabites also were a sect within Yahwism, and their way of life
was not a survival of earlier nomadism, but a deliberate attempt to
create an imagined ideal state of human life. Similar movements
could be found among modern Russian and American sects.

Elsewhere,[26] Winckler maintained that the idea of the changeless desert was also a mistaken assumption on the part of the
developmentalists. In fact, there had been vast climatic changes in
Arabia over the centuries, involving the progressive deterioration
in the climate, and the relentless expansion of the desert. Even in
historical times, it was possible that Arabia had supported a
flourishing population. Indeed, on the basis of Assyrian texts,

[26] For example in *Die Keilinschriften und das Alte Testament*, Berlin,
1903³, pp. 143 ff.

Winckler argued for the existence of a powerful North Arabian Kingdom of Musri in the age of the late Assyrian empire, and maintained that it was possible that the Exodus had been not from Egypt (Heb. *Miṣraim*) but from the North Arabian kingdom of Musri. In Britain, the North Arabian theory was also advocated by T. K. Cheyne.[27]

It must be acknowledged that among Winckler's wheat, there is a certain amount of chaff. The North Arabian theory is today discredited and the exaggerated claims of pan-Babylonianism have been rejected by subsequent scholarship. But we should not disregard Winckler's important methodological points. Above all, he was stressing that historical evidence is important in the interpretation of the cultural history of an area. The developmentalists were saying, in effect, that because we did not know the history of the desert regions in Arabia therefore they could not have had any history; we could therefore think of the desert as 'changeless' and assume that it had preserved elements of primitive Semitic religion from the earliest times to the present day. Winckler, on the other hand, was emphasizing that Israel had been surrounded by ancient flourishing civilizations in Mesopotamia and South Arabia, not to mention Egypt, and he was arguing that this evidence should be considered when assertions were made about the influences on ancient Israel. Further, we need to be reminded that discarded as the North Arabian theory may be, North Arabia itself remains largely unexcavated. So far, only surface explorations have been permitted, and these have been for limited periods only, often under difficult conditions.[28] Until full excavation of the area is possible, conclusions must remain

[27] T. K. Cheyne, *Traditions and Beliefs of Ancient Israel*, London, 1907. On this theory, as well as that of climatic change, see J. A. Montgomery, *Arabia and the Bible*, 1934, reprinted New York, 1969, pp. 94 ff. J. Henninger, *Über Lebensraum und Lebensformen der Frühsemiten* (Arbeitsgemeinschaft für Forschung des Landes Nordrhein-Westfalen, Nr. 151), Köln and Opladen, 1968, p. 10, note 11, summarizes recent study of the climate of the Near East, concluding that while small variations must be allowed for, there has been no fundamental climatic change in the region for the past 7,000 years. Since 2,400 B.C., the climate has been drier than during the period 5,000–2,400 B.C., but has essentially remained constant.

[28] For accounts of the most recent survey, together with discussions of previous explorations see F. V. Winnett and W. L. Reed, *Ancient Records from North Arabia*, Toronto, 1970.

tentative. Winckler's point remains, however, that lack of know
ledge of history does not mean no history. Also, Winckler's
diffusionism deserves close attention. Disregarding the excessive
claims of the pan-Babylonians about the extent of the diffusion of
culture all over the world from Babylon, it remains a fact that
primitive peoples are often fundamentally affected by contact
with 'higher' civilizations,[29] and that parts of the Arabian desert
had contact with Assyria and Babylon.[30] This alone is sufficient
to call into serious question the developmentalist view of societies
evolving through identical stages, and of the desert preserving
examples of those earliest stages. Finally, 'degeneration' of developed civilizations is well known, for example, from Central and
Southern America, and it is not impossible that much of what
seems to be primitive in Arabia, or in pre-Islamic religion, is in
fact a degeneration from earlier civilization.

These, then, were the principal criticisms, as well as the principal theses of the rival diffusionist school. At the close of the
chapter, the present state of the issues involved will be discussed,
because it is arguable that in Old Testament study, the methodological issues at stake have not been seen nearly so clearly in recent
times as they were at the beginning of the present century. For
the moment, however, it is necessary to consider one final criticism
of developmentalism and the doctrine of survivals.

Probably the most acute criticisms that were expressed against
the work of Robertson Smith at the time when his work was first
published, were those of the orientalist Theodor Nöldeke.[31]
Nöldeke's criticisms were general and particular. In his general
criticisms, he anticipated very clearly the position later to be
taken up by anthropologists of the third period in their attack on
the second period of anthropology. Nöldeke pointed out that if
one was going to reconstruct history on the basis of comparisons
of social data from various parts of the world, then the method
was impossible to control scientifically. Further, he was un-
convinced by Robertson Smith's use of data from North America
and Australia, and its application to ancient Arabia. 'We must not

---

[29] Keesing, *Cultural Anthropology*, pp. 143–4.
[30] See Trude Weiss-Rosmarin, *Aribi und Arabien in den Babylonisch-
Assyrischen Quellen*, Diss. Würzburg, 1931.
[31] Th. Nöldeke in *Zeitschrift der Deutschen Morgenländischen Gesellschaft*, 40 (1886), pp. 148–87. This is a review of *Kinship and Marriage*.

idealize these Arabs,' he wrote, 'but Robertson Smith is too inclined to regard them as utter barbarians and too readily applies to them analogies from North American Indians and aboriginal Australians.'[32] Nöldeke agreed with Robertson Smith that genealogies often reflected tribal history; but it was quite a different matter whether one could ever be in a position to know the original or earliest forms of ancient Semitic and Arab social life.

Nöldeke's particular criticisms were directed at Robertson Smith's interpretation of texts and passages from the Old Testament. It might be possible to argue etymologically that Leah and Rachel were animal names but what did this prove? The names Bilhah and Zilpah, the other two 'mothers' of the sons of Jacob, were not animal names, and neither were the overwhelming majority of Old Testament names. Again, the argument, from Gen. 48:5 ff.,[33] that children were reckoned to their mother's people and not their father's, ignored the context. In context, the purpose of the passage was to justify Ephraim and Manasseh taking their place alongside the other sons of Jacob as heads of tribes.

In these particular criticisms, Nöldeke had again anticipated the argument of later anthropologists against the doctrine of survivals. Robertson Smith had taken his evidence from the Old Testament and interpreted it not in terms of its actual context, but in terms of other evidence also taken out of context. Thus Gen. 2:24 says nothing about a man's residence after marriage. It expresses the fact that after marriage, a man's main affections and loyalties are transferred from his parents to his wife. Jacob's residence with his wives and father-in-law is an expedient made necessary by the enmity of his brother Esau. The incident in Gen. 34, where it is insisted that the sons of Hamor and Shechem are circumcised before they can marry Israelite women seems to have been from the outset a ruse to make it easier for the Israelites to overcome their potential enemies. While the Shechemites were recovering from their operation, they were easy prey for Simeon and Levi. One cannot rule out the possibility that the earliest Semitic social organization was matriarchal and matrilineal. However, it is questionable whether this could be proved on the basis of the evidence available, and it could not be proved by the sort of methods used by Robertson Smith.

[32] Nöldeke, p. 155 (translation mine).   [33] See above, p. 25.

We have spent some time, then, considering the positions
described in this chapter as developmentalist (backed by the
doctrine of survivals) and diffusionist (based on asserting the
importance of ancient Near Eastern historical texts). Before a
final judgement is passed, it is worth considering what influence
these two positions have had in more recent scholarship.

As a first example, we may take the book by Oesterley and
Robinson on Hebrew Religion.[34] This book is not today important;
but one has the impression that it is still read to some extent in
colleges and universities, and it must be pointed out here that any
implied criticisms of the book in what follows will only be criticisms of its early chapters. The book is concerned with the entire
history of Hebrew religion, and not just the beginnings, which
will be our particular concern here. From the outset, *Hebrew
Religion*, of which the second edition appeared in 1937, strikes one
as itself a survival from a past age of scholarship. Constant reference is made to Robertson Smith, Wellhausen, Curtiss, Frazer and
others from the second period of anthropology, and where newer
anthropological work is recognized, it is work mainly concerned
with theories about the nature of religion in general, and the
earliest forms of religion in particular. An interesting development
is that references are made to the Babylonian material; but it is
the Babylonian material interpreted so as to support developmentalism and the doctrine of survivals, not the diffusionist-
historical approach of the Winckler school. It is not the purpose
of the present book to describe the effect of anthropology on
assyriology; but it must always be remembered that there has
been such an influence, and that it has affected Old Testament
study when Babylonian material has been used as the key or
context for Old Testament interpretation. An obvious example
would be the way in which Frazer's theories of magic have
influenced the interpretation of Babylonian magical texts.

In the opening section of *Hebrew Religion*, the general religious
stages through which all peoples pass are defined *roughly* as pre-
animism, animism and polytheism. One recalls that Curtiss thought
that he had found evidence for animism in primitive Semitic
religion in the association of spirits with high places, wells and
trees, etc. The book describes the way in which, at the animistic

[34] W. O. E. Oesterley and T. H. Robinson, *Hebrew Religion. Its Origin
and Development*, London, 1930, 1937[2].

stage, trees, wells and stones, etc. are regarded as sacred, and there
follow sections which illustrate 'Remnants of Animism in Hebrew
Religion' under the headings of Sacred Trees, Sacred Waters,
Sacred Stones, Rocks and Mountains. The arguments from the
Old Testament are classical examples of the use of the doctrine of
survivals. Verses are plucked from their context, and then given
what to the writers are logical explanations in terms of animism.
This is then sufficient evidence for the animistic stage through
which the ancient Hebrews are supposed to have passed. Here is
an example:

> In Genesis 14:7 it is said that another name for Kadesh
> ('sanctuary') was *'En-mishpat'*, 'the spring of decision'. This
> name implies that it was a well to which men came in order to
> obtain a decision about some point of dispute; it is thus an
> oracle-well. It must therefore have been believed to be the abode
> of a spirit, a holy well, that is; and this is borne out by the name
> of the place in which it was situated, *Kadesh*, a 'sanctuary'.[35]

The argument here rests on a number of unproveable assumptions;
a 'spring of decision' *must have been* an oracle-well (as opposed to
a traditional place at which disputes were resolved by discussion
or adjudication); if it was an oracle-well it *must have been* believed
to be the abode of a spirit, and is thus evidence of animism. Such
inferences are typical of the 'discovery' and interpretation of
survivals to be found in many writers who practised the method.
    Later in the book,[36] the authors argued for a totemistic stage in
ancient Semitic society and religion, a stage shared by the ancient
ancestors of the Hebrews, and of which survivals could be found
in the Old Testament. Here, all the old arguments from Robertson
Smith's *Kinship and Marriage* were presented, including that of
the animal names of tribes, etc. Although Oesterley and Robinson
recognized that a few prominent scholars denied that remnants
of totemism were to be discerned in the Old Testament, the
opinion was given that their objections 'do not carry conviction.'[37]
It is astonishing that as late as 1937, eminent Old Testament
scholars could be reproducing anthropological arguments which
had long been rejected by professional anthropologists.

[35] *Hebrew Religion* (2nd ed.), p. 35.
[36] *Hebrew Religion*, pp. 62 ff.   [37] Op. cit., p. 66.

Another example can be taken from Albrecht Alt's essay *Der Gott der Väter*. Alt's essay, first published in 1929, has been the basis for much subsequent work on the Old Testament patriarchs, [38] and it is arguable that the whole essay is a rather sophisticated example of the use of the methods more crudely employed by Robertson Smith, Wellhausen and Curtiss. Briefly, Alt's argument is that phrases in the book of Genesis such as 'God of Abraham' (28:13), 'Fear (or Kinsman) of Isaac' (31:42) and 'Mighty One of Jacob' (49:24) should be understood in the light of inscriptions from roughly 50 B.C. to A.D. 350 which have been found in numerous parts of Arabia, but especially in areas that were part of the Nabatean kingdom. The inscriptions include phrases which talk about the 'God of X,' X being a man's name, and it is assumed that such phrases imply a type of religion in which X founded a religious cult, whereafter his posterity continued to worship the god whose name was indissolubly bound to that of their forebear, X. It is suggested by Alt that the phrases from Genesis should be understood in the same way, and that we should conclude that Abraham, Isaac and Jacob were founders of cults, and that their posterity worshipped the divine, under the name of the God of Abraham, etc. Alt hoped not only to recover a scrap of historicity for the patriarchs; he hoped to have discovered the type of religion practised by the Hebrew forebears at a time concerning which the Old Testament provides us with only scraps of evidence.

A closer look at Alt's argument suggests that it is based on the assumptions of the doctrine of survivals, and some sort of view of the unchanging desert. First, the phrases 'God of Abraham,' 'Fear of Isaac,' and 'Mighty One of Jacob' are taken out of context and interpreted in the light of similar phrases from inscriptions over 1,500 years later than the time of the patriarchs. Secondly, it is assumed that nomadic peoples living in the desert develop a distinctive type of religion, and that the desert preserves this intact, so that whether tribes emerge from the desert into contact with civilization in the first half of the second millennium B.C. or 1,500 years later, the same type of religion is being practised, and thus comparisons can be made. Thirdly, it is assumed that where we have the older, more extensive text of the Old Testament in

[38] A. Alt, *Der Gott der Väter*, in *BWANT* III, 12 (1929). Reprinted in *Kleine Schriften*, I, Munich, 1959, pp. 1–78. English translation in *Essays on Old Testament History and Religion*, Oxford, 1966.

which phrases like 'God of Abraham' occur, and much later, and
more fragmentary inscriptions in which there are similar phrases,
it is the former that must be understood in the light of the latter
and not vice versa. It is also interesting to note how close Alt is to
Curtiss, when he commends the Arabian evidence that he is using
because it comes from areas and from dates which preclude
Christian influence, i.e. which can be said more surely to be
evidence of something primitive. It is difficult to escape the conclusion that Alt has done what Robertson Smith and others did
before him, but instead of using the evidence of pre-Islamic
literary texts, or the accounts of travellers, he has turned to inscriptions. But the basic method, it can be argued, is unchanged.
To be sure, Alt has been criticized by some ancient Near Eastern
specialists for using, for the purposes of comparison, data which is
so much later than the Old Testament.[39] Instead, it has been
pointed out that the so-called Cappadocian texts of the nineteenth
century B.C. would provide examples closer in time to the Hebrew
patriarchs,[40] although Alt himself disallowed the usefulness of
these texts.[41] However, the appropriateness or otherwise of the
Cappadocian texts is not relevant to the main argument here,
which is that Alt's influential essay exhibits and keeps alive in
contemporary scholarship a particular type of method which
needs to be closely examined in its anthropological assumptions.

It is arguable that developmentalism and the doctrine of survivals also play their part in supporting another influential thesis,
namely, that the Passover festival originated from an apotropaic
rite of semi-nomadic stockbreeders.[42] The argument is based on
the observation that before semi-nomadic herdsmen in Arabia
move in spring from desert winter pasturage, to pasturage in the
more cultivated regions, they kill an animal and sprinkle its blood
in order to ward off evil powers. It is suggested that the ancient
forebears of the Hebrews carried out a similar procedure when they
were semi-nomadic herdsmen, and that this is the origin of the
Passover ritual. The association of this annual rite with the once-

[39] For example, K. A. Kitchen, *Ancient Orient and Old Testament*,
London, 1966, pp. 50–1.
[40] See the references in Kitchen, pp. 50–1.
[41] Alt, *Kleine Schriften*, I, p. 31, note 1.
[42] For example, M. Noth, *Exodus*, London, 1962, pp. 90–1; R. de Vaux,
Ancient Israel, London, 1961, p. 489.

for-all event of the Exodus would result from associating a regular 'departure' from certain pastures, with the 'departure' par excellence, that from Egypt.

The difficulties raised by the Passover narratives should in no way be minimized, and in view of the many eminent scholars of different persuasions who hold something like the position out-lined above, the suggestion should not be written off lightly. It should be noted, however, that the method involved in the argument certainly displays some of the features of the use of the doctrine of survivals. The Old Testament accounts of the killing of the lamb and the shedding of its blood are separated from the main context, and then interpreted in the light of evidence which, though modern, is assumed to reflect what semi-nomads have *always* done when moving from one pasture to another in the spring. Purely at the level of method, it seems to the present writer that Segal's approach to the origin of the Passover rite is on firmer ground.[43] Segal compares elements of the Passover as described in Exod. 12–13 (e.g. the wearing of festival garments, Exod. 12:35, the dedication of firstborn children, Exod. 13:2) with new-year rites described in ancient Near Eastern accounts. He concludes that the Passover originated in a new-year ceremony observed by the Israelite slaves in Egypt. Although Segal's com-parative method can be no substitute for proper historical evidence, at least it is not based upon questionable anthropological assump-tions. H. H. Rowley makes a salutary point in his treatment of the Passover.[44] He is aware that numerous theories have been advanced about the origin of the Passover, but he points out that none of the 'original meanings' of the Passover that these theories imply, find any reference in the Old Testament. The evidence at our dis-posal permits us only to see what the Passover meant in the context of the worship and faith of ancient Israel.

I have suggested, then, that arguments based on the doctrine of survivals are not at all absent from contemporary Old Testament study, even if the method is not explicitly recognized as such. What about its rival, diffusionism? Until the time of his death, Professor S. H. Hooke was probably the principal Old Testament scholar who embraced, or had embraced, a full diffusionist posi-tion, and this because he had studied under anthropologists in

[43] J. B. Segal, *The Hebrew Passover*, Oxford, 1963.
[44] H. H. Rowley, *Worship in Ancient Israel*, London, 1967, pp. 49–50.

Manchester at the time of the so-called heliocentric school, which claimed that Egyptian culture had been diffused far and wide all over the world.[45] Hooke looked more to Babylon than to Egypt as a centre from which culture had been diffused, and although he is probably best known for his advocacy of the myth and ritual position, his diffusionism was made plain in several writings. For example, he maintained that alleged traces of primitive Semitic religion among contemporary or pre-Islamic Arabs were not survivals, but degenerations from a culture pattern. 'The Arab religious customs, the sacred nature of stones, trees, wells, mountains . . . must be regarded rather as the *membra disjecta*, the relics of a pattern with which the nomad peoples were once in contact but have now lost.'[46] He interpreted the Passover, not as a primitive apotropaic rite, but as a degeneration from an element of the Babylonian New Year festival;[47] and he traced the influence of the Epic of Gilgamesh not only to the Elijah stories of the Old Testament, but as far afield as Melanesia.[48]

As far as I am aware, there is no work that is currently being undertaken in Old Testament study which has such a definite diffusionist bias as did the writings of the pan-Babylonians, or Hooke. Rather, one gets the impression that the issues of the methodological clash between the developmentalists and the diffusionists have become blurred in recent scholarship. The importance of the Babylonian and other similar material has, of course, been recognized on all fronts; yet, Arabic material has also continued to be used.[49] If Old Testament scholars have used a

---

[45] Keesing, *Cultural Anthropology*, pp. 148–9.

[46] S. H. Hooke, 'The Mixture of Cults in Canaan,' in *The Siege Perilous*, London, 1956, p. 254 (the essay dates from 1931). The use of the word 'relics' by both Hooke and Robertson Smith (see p. 25) must not lead us to think that they were saying the same thing. For Robertson Smith, the 'relics' were survivals from primitive Semitic religion; for Hooke, they were fragmented remains of a pattern of civilization which had once dominated the ancient Near East.

[47] Hooke, *Myth and Ritual*, London, 1933, p. 12.

[48] Hooke, 'Some Parallels with the Gilgamesh Story,' in *The Siege Perilous* (this essay dates from 1934).

[49] In *The Desert Bible. Nomadic Tribal Culture and Old Testament Interpretation*, London, 1974, M. S. Seale has criticized Old Testament scholarship for paying too much attention to ancient Near Eastern texts, and too little attention to pre-Islamic Arabic poetry. This is virtually a modern re-statement of parts of Robertson Smith's position.

cultural model, whether consciously or unconsciously, it has been one in which centres of civilization like Babylon, Egypt, Ugarit and the Palestinian city states have been seen as generating spheres of cultural influence; but these spheres of influence have not covered the entire ancient Near East. There have been numerous (desert) 'gaps,' and in these 'gaps' peoples like the forebears of the ancient Hebrews are thought to have lived, largely untouched by the higher cultures of the area, so that it remains legitimate to deduce social and religious facts about such ancient forebears by comparisons with later peoples such as Bedouin tribes, who similarly, so the model would presuppose, have had minimal contact with advanced cultures, and historical events. Whether this is adequate in the light of the evidence available is something that cultural anthropologists could perhaps tell Old Testament specialists.

I propose to conclude this chapter by summarizing recent anthropological discussion on some of the central topics of method that have been mentioned above.

The Concept of Nomadism

Old Testament study continues to employ the concepts of 'nomadism' and 'semi-nomadism,' and to base conclusions about the ancient Hebrews on the use of these concepts.[50] By way of contrast, recent anthropological study has doubted the value of classifying peoples as 'nomadic.'[51] Perhaps N. Dyson-Hudson is unduly pessimistic when he asserts in his introduction to *Perspectives on Nomadism*

that the simple if somewhat gloomy truth is that we really know extraordinarily little about human behaviour in nomadic societies. Certainly much of what passes for knowledge about

[50] See, for example, R. de Vaux, *Histoire ancienne d'Israël*, Vol. I, Paris, 1971, pp. 220 ff; E.T., *The Early History of Israel*, London, 1978, pp. 221 ff., esp. pp. 231–2.

[51] W. Irons and N. Dyson-Hudson (eds.), *Perspectives on Nomadism*, Leiden, 1972, especially the articles 'The Study of Nomads' by N. Dyson-Hudson, and 'The Status of Nomadism as a Cultural Phenomenon in the Middle East' by B. Spooner.

nomads (inside or outside the anthropological profession) is
quite misleading[52]

but towards the end of this essay, he questions the notion of
nomadism itself. 'Nomadism,' he argues, is nothing more than the
overlap between two quite distinct sets of phenomena, livestock
breeding and spatial mobility, and each of these sets of phenomena
embraces factors quite beyond what is popularly understood by
'nomadism.' These two sets of phenomena have been arbitrarily
'yoked together,' with the result that misleading assumptions have
been made, for example, in the common belief that nomadic movement is caused simply by environmental factors. Limiting himself to the livestock breeding side of 'nomadism,' Dyson-Hudson
lists eight areas in which we need to have specific information if
we are to begin to understand even one type of nomadic society.
These include the type of livestock, the number of livestock, their
grazing characteristics in relation to the herbage available, the
human population's degree of dependence on livestock, and its
degree of commitment to livestock. The writer concludes:

> we are dealing with variables; and as soon as we break down the
> category of 'nomadism' into even its immediate constituents of
> herding and movement, and of these choose one, we are faced
> with dozens of variables which admit of virtually infinite re-
> combination. Until we possess precise knowledge on such
> matters, we cannot claim adequate knowledge of even a single
> nomadic society—let alone 'nomadism' as some more general
> form of human experience.[53]

It needs to be borne in mind that Dyson-Hudson is here writing
about societies that can be observed; he is asking whether the
concept of nomadism is a useful one by means of which to describe
certain contemporary societies, and to make generalizations about
them, and comparisons between them. If a modern anthropologist
is so sceptical about the idea of 'nomadism' in regard to observable
societies, how much more cautious should Old Testament scholars
be when dealing with ancient societies attested only by fragmentary historical records. In view of Dyson-Hudson's remarks,
it may not be going too far to say that Old Testament study should

[52] *Perspectives on Nomadism*, p. 2.   [53] Op. cit., p. 26.

abandon the procedure whereby societies have been lumped together under the umbrella of 'nomads' or 'semi-nomads' for the purposes of comparison and historical reconstruction; or at least it should be made clear that until anthropologists have made greater progress towards establishing satisfactory criteria for the study of 'nomadic' societies, Old Testament scholars should always indicate when they speak about nomads or semi-nomads that much less can be known about such peoples than has usually been assumed.

Evolution and Diffusion

It can be stated with reasonable certainty that although anthropologists continue to argue the merits of evolution versus diffusion, they would be agreed that their respective positions are *theories* which seek to interpret in general outline the available evidence about similarities of material culture, social organization, and beliefs among peoples. Neither view would begin to attempt to *reconstruct* the cultural history of a *single* society which can be observed today, let alone one which we know about only from partial historical records.[54] Thus, the committed evolutionist will argue for a *general* evolution of mankind from more simple to more complex forms of culture, but will recognize many variations and complexities, within the general movement, for which terms such as 'multilinear evolution' and 'differential evolution' have been coined.[55]

The continuing weakness of evolutionism as an explanation of culture development and similarity is that it can tend to treat societies as systems isolated from each other, implying that inventions that have been crucial to cultural progress have been made independently in different societies. In fact, it is almost

[54] H. E. Driver, 'Cross-Cultural Studies' in *Handbook of Social and Cultural Anthropology*, p. 356. 'It should be remembered, however, that if enough evolutionary detail were known about each of a thousand societies, we would have a hard time indeed finding two of them that evolved through exactly the same sequence for a thousand or so items of culture. . . . All that evolutionary postdictions from synchronic nonmaterial culture can show is the very broad general trend of societies as a whole.'

[55] R. L. Carneiro, 'The Four Faces of Evolution' in *Handbook of Social and Cultural Anthropology*, pp. 101–8.

DA

certain that there was a single origin for the alphabet, and that the
discovery of important metals and the domestication of important
foods such as corn were 'inventions' made at the most only several
times, after which the inventions spread by diffusion to the vast
majority of societies possessing them at any given time.[56] However,
although the diffusionist may have some success in tracing the
spread of material culture where historical evidence or material
remains make this possible, he is sceptical about doing this with
confidence in the case of social organizations or beliefs. Thus,
H. E. Driver writes, 'for nonmaterial variables describing human
behaviour, which leave no physical evidence for the archaeologist
to unearth and the modern scientific laboratory to test, little is
known about their evolution, history or causal relationships.'[57] As
in the case of 'nomadism,' then, we see that recent anthropological
work on the history of culture has shown that matters are far more
complicated than has been supposed in Old Testament study, and
that in the absence of historical evidence, anthropology can no
longer fill out the gaps in our knowledge of the earliest history of
the Hebrews, by providing generalized theories of cultural history
that can be applied to a single society.

A final word should be said with regard to the notion of
'bedouin.' I am not aware of a recent anthropological discussion
of the meaning and usefulness of this term, but my own reading
of recent historical discussions of the history of 'nomadism' and
bedouin in the ancient Near East leads me to suspect that this may
be another term which must be used with caution.[58] Etymologically speaking, 'bedouin' means 'dwellers of the desert,' and
the term has often been used interchangeably with 'nomad.'
Dostal[59] has defined bedouin as 'tribes of dromedary-shepherds
who are at the same time rider-warriors. Their economic structure
is characterized by the keeping of very large flocks, while their
social structure is founded on the notion of descent from common
ancestors.' However, discussions of the history of 'bedouinism'

---

[56] Driver, op. cit., p. 350.   [57] Op. cit., p. 350.

[58] See especially F. Gabrieli (ed.), *L'antica societa beduina*, Studi
Semitici, 2, Rome, 1959; W. Caskel, *Die Bedeutung der Beduinen in der
Geschichte der Araber*, (Arbeitsgemeinschaft für Forschung des Landes
Nordrhein-Westfalen, 8), Köln, 1953; J. Henninger, *Über Lebensraum
und Lebensformen der Frühsemiten*.

[59] W. Dostal, 'The Evolution of Bedouin Life' in *L'antica societata
beduina*, pp. 14–15.

seem to lack terminological precision. For example, given Dostal's definition of 'bedouin' quoted above, and the agreement that 'bedouinism proper' is not to be found until the third century A.D.,[60] it is dificult to see how it is possible to write about 'ancient bedouin society' at all, unless the meaning of 'ancient' is somewhat stretched. In fact, Dostal avoids the charge of inconsistency by positing a 'proto-bedouin' and a 'full bedouin' period, and Henninger is able to find evidence from the Old Testament for the existence of bedouin by implying the definition: bedouin equals warlike nomads.[61] It would seem that scholarly discussion is badly in need of a careful evaluation of the definition and value of the term 'bedouin.'

[60] Caskel, op. cit., pp. 15 ff.; Henninger, op. cit., p. 17; R. de Vaux, *Histoire ancienne d'Israël*, I, p. 214; E.T., p. 222.

[61] Henninger, op. cit., p. 17, and Henninger in *L'antica societa beduina*, pp. 84–5.

3

Primitive Mentality

In the opening chapter,[1] it was pointed out that as long ago as the latter part of the eighteenth century, an attempt was made to interpret Old Testament narratives with the help of a theory of primitive mentality which was based on accounts of how modern 'primitives' thought. The use of theories of primitive mentality has continued in Old Testament study to the present day, and could be defended in the following way: we are separated from the ancient Hebrews by a vast gap of time and culture. The Hebrews described in the Old Testament lived mostly before the foundations of modern science began to be laid by the Greeks and they must have viewed the world in a very different way from ourselves. The modern scholar will be in danger of mis-interpreting the Old Testament if he does not make allowances for the different world-view of the ancient Hebrews compared with ourselves and he may get some help in understanding how ancient Hebrews thought if he considers how the world is viewed by contemporary 'primitives' who have a pre-scientific outlook on the world.

In this chapter we shall consider three attempts to explain the thought processes of primitives, and we shall see how the three explanations have been used in Old Testament study. The three explanations have a number of things in common. To begin with, they are all dependent on the same sort of pre-fieldwork information about the lives of primitives. The characteristic thing about this information is that it suggests that primitives experience the world in a way very different from modern Western peoples, and in this sense, it calls for some sort of explanation. The reader may well be familiar with the sort of evidence that is relevant here, and

[1] See above, p. 7.

if not, examples of it can be found, for example, in Frazer's *The Golden Bough*.[2] Typical are stories which suggest that primitives cannot distinguish between dreams and their waking experiences; which suggest that primitives believe that evil men can, while asleep, roam abroad in the form of dangerous wild animals. Then there are the familiar stories about magic that is practised by making images of people, or by destroying hair or nail clippings of the victim; or stories about the reluctance of primitives to disclose their name to strangers apparently for fear that the strangers will get power over them. It is not surprising that as attempts at explanation of the same sort of phenomena, the three views should have a certain overlap. But they also have significant differences, which will be emphasized at the appropriate points. These differences should at least be a warning that the explanation of such evidence about primitives is by no means a simple matter.

The first explanation to be considered will be Sir James Frazer's theory of the workings of primitive magic.[3] As is well known, Frazer divided the intellectual and mental development of all mankind into roughly three stages—the stages of magic, religion, and science. Religion was distinguished by its concern with spiritual forces or personalities. Magic and science had this in common, that they did not resort to the supernatural, but were both based on belief in the workings of inexorable laws of nature. The difference between magic and science was that in the former, the laws were based on mistaken observation; mistaken, that is, when compared with what man has subsequently learned from science about the laws which govern the relations of objects in the physical world. Nonetheless, magic had a logic of its own, and Frazer's aim was to describe this logic, and thus make sense of the accounts of the behaviour of primitives which were so surprising to the modern reader.

Frazer distinguished between homoeopathic or imitative magic, and contagious magic. The former was based on what Frazer called the Law of Similarity, which was the (mistaken) belief that things sharing a common property (e.g. shape or colour) could influence each other. Examples of this type of magic would be the making of a representation of a person whom one wished to harm,

[2] J. G. Frazer, *The Golden Bough*. Reference will be made to the Abridged Edition, London, 1957 (paperback).
[3] For what follows, see Frazer, op. cit., pp. 14–109.

or the imitation of the patterns of a cloud in a rain-making dance. By harming the representation, one would be harming the actual person; by simulating the rain clouds, one would produce rain. Contagious magic, on the other hand, depended on the Law of Contact. This law expressed the belief of primitives that things which had once been in contact with each other were thereafter in some way always in contact. Therefore, hair, or nail clippings, or an extracted tooth were still in some way part of the person from whom they came, and the destruction of such things would harm that person.

This brief description of Frazer's position has necessarily involved over-simplification; but it does, I believe, do justice to the salient points. If it is now asked how Frazer knew that this was how primitives 'thought' when practising magic, it must be replied that his theory was not based on any first-hand experience of primitives and the magic that they practised. The position was based rather on a learned attempt to understand how a primitive might come to believe that he would be harmed if one of his teeth were to fall into the hands of an enemy. Further, this learned attempt was essentially a reading back of Frazer's intellectual and scientific background into a totally different situation; what seemed *to him*, given his particular background, to be a logical explanation for the practice of magic by primitives was supposed to represent the actual state of mind of the primitives.

Before I give some examples of the use of arguments in Old Testament study based on Frazer's view of magic, I shall try to show how recent anthropological study has interpreted magic. In the first place, although the word 'magic' continues to be used in many anthropological writings, the terms 'religion' and 'magic' are not regarded as adequate for describing types of social behaviour. *Notes and Queries on Anthropology* distinguishes between religion and magic in a way similar to Frazer's approach, by defining religion as presuming the existence of spiritual beings, and magic as not presupposing the necessary existence of such beings, but it warns us that 'often there is no clear separation in the ideas and practices of the simpler people between the two classes of beliefs.'[4] It continues, 'there is no agreement among anthropologists on the use of the terms "magic" and "religion," so that these words cannot be relied upon as technical terms'; however, it is

---

[4] *Notes and Queries on Anthropology*, p. 174.

possible to identify 'a body of behaviour which may be called magico-religious.' How 'religion' is to be defined, would appear to be a continuing discussion in anthropology;[5] a recent discussion of what Frazer would have called 'magic' is considered under the broader category of 'symbolic instrumentation.'[6]

If we consider further what is meant by 'symbolic instrumentation' we meet the criticism of Frazer that in his description of magic, he concentrated only on actions which seemed to be aimed at producing changes in the physical world, such as producing rain, making crops grow, or curing illnesses. Many recent writers[7] would argue that such activities must be understood as part of a larger class of activities, including marriage, initiation, and rites (including sacrificial rites) designed to restore broken relationships, and to assist in the maintenance of existing relationships, and the ongoing life of the community. Symbolic instrumentation is a way of enabling an individual or a society to express what could not otherwise be put into words; it makes explicit some of the values and hopes implicit in a society and shared by its members. In turn, the expression of these hopes and values in a symbolic objective way helps to reinforce them for the individual and the society.[8] On the face of it, there seems to be little in common between what Frazer called 'magic,' and, say, initiation and marriage rites. The interpretation of these activities considered together is made possible by the opinion of modern anthropology that Frazer was incorrect to regard magic as a crude form of science based on inadequate knowledge of causal 'laws.' This can be illustrated by two examples.

In his account of the religion of the Dinka, Lienhardt describes

[5] See M. E. Spiro, 'Religion: Problems of Definition and Explanation' in M. Banton (ed.), *Anthropological Approaches to the Study of Religion*, London, 1966, pp. 85–126.

[6] Nancy D. Munn, 'Symbolism in a Ritual Context' in *Handbook of Social and Cultural Anthropology*, pp. 592–3.

[7] See Nancy D. Munn, op. cit., p. 593, and the whole chapter 'Symbolic Action' in G. Lienhardt, *Divinity and Experience. The Religion of the Dinka*, Oxford, 1961.

[8] I have tried to put into my own words the following highly technical sentence from Nancy D. Munn, op. cit., p. 593. 'Ritual symbols release the relevant shared meanings embedded in the cultural code into the level of ongoing social process; through this objectivication they can come to "work back" upon the individual imagination with the authority of external reality.'

the practice of *thuic*, the knotting of a piece of grass, as, for example, in the enclosing of a stone that represents a lion in a knotted piece of grass, so that the lion will be killed. Lienhardt argues that to describe this as 'imitative magic' is to misunderstand the whole context of the activity. The symbolic act is no substitute for the serious business of hunting the lion, neither do the Dinka think that by performing such actions they have already assured the results that they desire. The action is, in fact, 'an external, physical representation of a well-formed mental intention. (The man concerned) has produced a model of his desires and hopes, upon which to base renewed practical endeavour.'[9] If this is accepted, the link between *thuic* and other less 'magical' activity is established as follows:

> The objects which the Dinka have in mind when knotting grass as we have described might, were the circumstances different, be achieved in some purely technical way. The principle involved, however, is similar to that which obtains in symbolic action in situations which, by their very nature, preclude the possibility of technical or practical action as a complete alternative. In the ceremonies for cleansing people of incest, for death, and for peace making which we now describe, what the symbolic action is intended to control is primarily a set of mental and moral dispositions. . . .[10]

The second example of a recent interpretation of magic in terms very different from those of Frazer, comes from S. J. Tambiah.[11] Tambiah argues that at the basis of magic there is a 'persuasive analogy' based upon a recognition of the similarities and differences between things. For example, the Azande treatment for leprosy is the application of the *araka* creeper to the affected limbs. Apparently, at a period in its growth, the creeper loses its leaves, which are replaced by 'a double row of bands, joined to the stalks, which little by little dry, split, and fall in small pieces' in the way that the extremities of limbs are affected in leprosy. However, with the creeper, this decay is the prelude to new growth. The use of the *araka* creeper in the treatment of leprosy, then, is not based upon

[9] Lienhardt, op. cit., pp. 282–3.   [10] Op. cit., p. 283.
[11] S. J. Tambiah, 'Form and Meaning of Magical Acts: A point of View' in R. Horton and Ruth Finnegan (eds.), *Modes of Thought*, London, 1973, pp. 199–229.

faulty observation by the Azande; rather, the treatment expresses the hope that just as with the creeper, so with the leper, the falling away of the extremity of limbs will be a prelude to recovery. Tambiah argues that this view of what is implied in magical acts is capable of wide application.[12]

The interpretation of magic in terms which avoid Frazer's laws of similarity and contact enable modern anthropologists to allow that for vast areas of their lives, 'primitives' have a very good idea of what causes what in their environment. Frazer seems to have been in danger of ignoring these areas of life, and of creating the impression that 'primitives' believed all the time that like was affecting like; but as one writer has put it, 'Nobody in their senses could possibly believe that all things that share some common quality, and all things that have once been in contact, are continually affecting one another; in a world so conceived almost everything would all the time be affecting almost everything else, and all would be chaos. Magicians and their clients know quite well that for most of the time like is *not* affecting like.'[13]

The whole discussion can be summed up as follows. There is no such thing as a magical world-view. Symbolic actions are performed in order to help an individual express and renew his desires and intentions,[14] they are performed in situations of doubt and uncertainty,[15] they are performed in situations such as death, peace-making, where no alternative practical or technical action could be carried out. They may be based on a 'persuasive analogy'; they are certainly expressive of hopes and values for the individual and the community. Although the matter cannot be further explored here, symbolic action thus understood is also practised in modern Western societies.

It is now our task to see how far Frazer's theories of magic have

---

[12] Tambiah, op. cit., pp. 214 ff.

[13] J. Beattie, *Other Cultures*, London, 1966, p. 206.

[14] Lienhardt, op. cit., p. 283.

[15] Beattie, op. cit., p. 207, 'Malinowski's Trobriand Islanders carry out a number of magical rites before they set out on long and hazardous kula voyages, but they do not bother with magic when they are simply going for a day's fishing on the lagoon. This is just what we should expect. There are grave dangers to be faced on ocean voyages in fragile canoes: the sheltered lagoon is free from hazard. And where there are good grounds for anxiety, to relieve it may be an important function of magic activity.'

affected Old Testament study, and at the outset, it must be
admitted that it is not an easy matter to demonstrate its influence
in recent writing. This is because Frazer's explanations have
become so much a part of what many people think about the
workings of magic, that almost all the modern textbooks on the
Old Testament which speak of magic do not even bother to define
the term magic.[16] One must also be fair to Old Testament scholars,
and point out that if they find magic in the Old Testament, it is
usually remains or traces of magical belief that they find; or they
argue that the practice of magic was most common among the
poorest peasant classes in ancient Israel. The majority of writers
draw a sharp distinction between the official attitude of Israelite
religion towards magic, which is a hostile attitude, and the religious
practices of Israel's neighbours, which are seen to have been
basically much more magical. It is also necessary to emphasize
that modern writers on the Old Testament do not suggest that
Israelite mentality in ancient times was characterized by Frazer's
laws of similarity and contact. However, it is difficult to escape the
conclusion that where recent Old Testament writers do mention
magic, they imply that there is such a thing as a magical outlook
which dominates a society's whole experience of the world.
Almost certainly, such writers do not allow for the possibility that
magical rites may not be causative but expressive, and their
description of magic often implies an intellectual or psychological,
rather than a sociological, understanding of the phenomenon.
A good example is contained in Fohrer's book on Israelite religion.
Fohrer distinguishes 'the magical approach to life' from several
other 'approaches to life' and describes the former as follows:

> In Palestinian Israel the magical approach was primarily shaped
> by the Canaanite vegetation and fertility cults whose basis was
> largely magical. Only in the conceptual world of magic can one
> expect to strengthen the deity and maintain the mysterious force
> of life by means of sexual rites, or to reawaken the rhythm of
> nature each year and render the earth fertile through rites

[16] The reader can check this from the standard books on Hebrew or
Israelite religion, or the standard Old Testament theologies. An exception
is in the first volume of von Rad's Theology, where magical thought is
explicitly described as a total world-view. See *Theologie des Alten Testaments*, Vol. I, Munich, 1962⁴, p. 47. E.T. *Old Testament Theology*, Vol. I,
Edinburgh, 1962, p. 34.

centering on a deity that fades away and then revives. Therefore, the Israelites adopted many Canaanite magical practices.[17]

There is much in Fohrer's overall discussion with which I have no quarrel, such as his insistence that magical practices in ancient Israel were used in situations of uncertainty or anxiety, or the Old Testament passages he cites as possible evidence for magical practices. However, the quotation above makes clear Fohrer's belief that the Canaanite cults were necessarily causal, and that they imply a conceptual world of magic. It is precisely these points that modern anthropological discussions of Frazer have questioned, and it is not stating too much to argue that there is a need in Old Testament research to see how far commonly-held views about magic in Old Testament study need to be modified in the light of recent anthropological work.

One of the criticisms of Frazer, it will be remembered, was that his explanation had been too intellectualist, and that it had been based on an application of modern logic and mental processes to primitive societies. The second attempt to explain information about primitives which we shall consider, that of the French sociologist L. Lévy-Bruhl, rejected such explanations by 'the English School'[18] and attempted instead a sociological explanation.[19] When a person is born, he is born into a particular society, and that society has a distinctive language, organization, institutions, and beliefs. From the first, the individual is moulded by these things, and he takes over from the society into which he is born a distinctive way of understanding and experiencing the world. Thus, according to Lévy-Bruhl, if we are to understand how a primitive regards, for example, magic, we must not try to explain his intellectual reasoning; we must examine what

[17] G. Fohrer, *Geschichte der israelitischen Religion*, Berlin, 1969, pp. 148 ff., E.T., *History of Israelite Religion*, London, 1973, pp. 155–6.

[18] Evans-Pritchard, 'Lévy-Bruhl's Theory of Primitive Mentality' (1933), reprinted in *Journal of the Anthropological Society of Oxford*, I, 1970, pp. 39–60, summarizes Lévy-Bruhl's criticism thus: 'The English School make the mistake of trying to explain social facts by processes of individual thought, and, worse still, by analogy with their own patterns of thought which are the product of different environmental conditions from those which have moulded the minds they seek to understand' (p. 39).

[19] Lévy-Bruhl's position is stated in *Les fonctions mentales dans les sociétés inférieures*, Paris, 1910; E.T., *How Natives Think*, London, 1926.

Lévy-Bruhl called his 'collective representations' (i.e. the language, institutions and beliefs of his society which contribute to his understanding of magic).

In theory, Lévy-Bruhl's position entails that there can be as many 'mentalities' as there are societies, but, in practice, Lévy-Bruhl apparently did not try to co-ordinate his explanations of primitive mentality with the 'collective representations' of primitives,[20] and he posited a uniform stage of a pre-logical mentality through which peoples passed. However, in describing primitive mentality as pre-logical, Lévy-Bruhl did not imply that it was illogical from the primitive point of view. Given the social conditioning of his 'collective representations,' the primitive was only capable of responding to certain sense impressions to the exclusion of others. None the less, his perception was subject to certain 'laws,' important among which was the law of mystical participation. According to this law, primitives perceived certain things as being mystically connected with other things, and this was why, if his child was ill, a father might drink the medicine that was intended for the child; or a man might not be able to see his shadow without at the same time believing that it was his soul.[21] There was also a blurring (from the modern standpoint) of the boundaries between objects, so that a man's personality could merge with that of his child; or his name, his shadow or his hair cuttings could be thought of as an extension of his personality. The similarity between Lévy-Bruhl's law of mystical participation and Frazer's law of contagion, in respect, for example, of hair cuttings, will be obvious. But it must not be forgotten that the presuppositions of the approaches of Frazer and Lévy-Bruhl were quite different, and that although no modern writer would want to try to describe primitives in the way Frazer did, the view that primitives can only be understood in terms of the total range of influences which their society brought to bear on them is still a widely-held view.[22] Lévy-Bruhl is criticized because in effect, he did not practise what he preached.

[20] Evans-Pritchard in *Jnl. of the Anthrop. Soc. of Oxford*, I, p. 40.

[21] These two examples are taken from Evans-Pritchard, *Theories of Primitive Religion*, Oxford, 1965, pp. 85–6.

[22] See the article and discussion 'Understanding in Philosophical Anthropology,' A. Hanson and P. Heelas in *Jnl. of the Anthrop. Soc. of Oxford*, I, 1970, pp. 61–81.

Many of the criticisms directed at Frazer apply also, however, to Lévy-Bruhl. He concentrated on those areas of life which were unusual, and not representative of primitives; he brought together examples regardless of social context and background; he over-emphasized the mystical nature of the life of primitives and under-emphasized similar facets in modern Western life. According to Evans-Pritchard, if Lévy-Bruhl's theories were true 'we would scarcely be able to communicate with primitives, even to learn their languages. The single fact that we can do so shows that Lévy-Bruhl was making too strong a contrast between the primitive and the civilized.'[23]

However, the influence of Lévy-Bruhl in Old Testament studies has been considerable. In 1911, H. Wheeler Robinson introduced the notion of 'corporate personality' into Old Testament studies,[24] and although in the first instance he was influenced by Sir Henry Maine's *Ancient Law* and the writings of Spencer and Gillen on Australian aborigines, the writings of Lévy-Bruhl later became the principal source for the basis and extension of the notion of corporate personality. Elsewhere,[25] I have argued that as used by Wheeler Robinson, corporate personality was ambiguous, and meant at least two things—corporate responsibility and corporate representation, to use Robinson's own terminology. Corporate responsibility was most directly dependent on Maine, and it was used to explain real problems in the Old Testament, such as why it was that the whole of Achan's family was put to death, according to Joshua 7, when sin had been committed only by Achan himself. Corporate representation owed much to Lévy-Bruhl's law of mystical participation, and tended to be applied to the Old Testament in passages where there was really no need for such explanation.

Briefly, the main burden of corporate representation was that Hebrew mentality, like Lévy-Bruhl's primitive mentality, did not

[23] Evans-Pritchard, *Theories of Primitive Religion*, p. 87. See also J. Cazeneuve, *Lucien Lévy-Bruhl*, E.T., Oxford, 1972, and the *Notebooks on Primitive Mentality*, E.T., Oxford, 1976, which contain Lévy-Bruhl's abandonment of some of the positions that he advocated, e.g. pre-logical mentality and the law of participation.

[24] H. W. Robinson, *The Christian Doctrine of Man*, Edinburgh, 1911, p. 8.

[25] See my article, 'The Hebrew Conception of Corporate Personality: A Re-Examination' in *J.T.S.*, XXI, 1970, pp. 1–16.

distinguish clearly between what the modern mind would regard as separate objects. In particular, there was a fluidity about the limits to a person's individuality, so that a personality might merge with that of a larger group to which an individual belonged, or might merge with other personalities in the group. One of Wheeler Robinson's most influential uses of the theory was in connection with the understanding of the Suffering Servant in Deutero-Isaiah. In the face of contradicting views in Old Testament study about the identity of the servant, some of which regarded the servant as an individual while others championed a corporate interpretation, Wheeler Robinson said in effect that both views could be correct, if one took account of the distinctive Hebrew view of personality.

There is a fluidity of conception, a possibility of swift transition from the one to the many, and vice versa, to which our thought and language have no real parallel. When we do honour today to the 'Unknown Warrior' we can clearly distinguish between the particular soldier buried in the Abbey and the great multitude of whom we have consciously made him the representative. But that clearness of distinction would have been lacking to an earlier world, prior to the development of the modern sense of personality.[26]

In order to avoid misunderstanding, I must make it clear that if I criticize Wheeler Robinson for propounding a theory of Hebrew mentality based on what I would maintain are untenable anthropological assumptions, I also accept that parts of the Old Testament appear to imply what might be called a 'corporate' sense of an individual figure or speaker. A well-known example is the 'I' of the psalms, where the speaker in the first person singular seems to be, or to represent, the whole people of Israel. I have argued elsewhere[27] that examples of the same thing can be found in modern experience, and that in order to understand them, there is no need for a special theory of Hebrew mentality. It seems to me that the onus is upon scholars who continue to talk of corporate personality to define what they mean, and to say upon

[26] H. W. Robinson, *The Cross in the Old Testament*, London, 1955, p. 77.
[27] In *J.T.S.*, XXI, 1970, pp. 12 ff.

what it is based if it implies a Hebrew mentality different from our own.

As a second example of the influence of Lévy-Bruhl's theories in Old Testament study, we may refer to the way in which A. R. Johnson has used the notion of 'extension of personality' in his writings. Johnson is confessedly dependent on Lévy-Bruhl for this notion,[28] and he applies it in an interesting way in the interpretation of the activities of messengers. Of the passage in Judges 11:12 ff.

> And Jephthah sent messengers unto the king of the children of Ammon, saying, What have I to do with thee, that thou art come to me to fight against my land . . .

Johnson writes, 'Through the agency of his messengers Jephthah . . . is regarded as being present—"in person." ' In other words, the *malakim* ('messengers'), as 'extensions' of their master's personality, are treated as actually *being* and not merely as representing their *'adon* ('lord').[29] There are numerous other examples, such as Elisha's staff, which is carried by Gehazi ahead of the prophet for the purpose of restoring to life the son of the Shunammite woman. The staff is assumed to be an extension of Elisha's personality.[30] The difficulty with explanations such as these is that they seem to be plausible enough, and can be neither proved nor disproved. That is why it becomes important to look for the underlying presuppositions of such interpretations, and to ask whether they can be checked. In the case of presuppositions based on anthropology, negative checks are possible. In connection with the interpretation of Judges 11:12 ff., it should be noted that more recent scholarship has interpreted the incident fruitfully in terms of the so-called messenger formula, and without recourse to theories of extension of personality.[31]

As a third example of the influence of Lévy-Bruhl's theories in Old Testament study, we may consider the use of the concept of 'corporate personality' (in the sense of corporate representation)

[28] A. R. Johnson, *The One and the Many in the Israelite Conception of God*, Cardiff, 1961[2], p. 2., n. 4.

[29] Op. cit., p. 6.

[30] Op. cit., pp. 6–7, on II Kings 4:29.

[31] See C. Westermann, *Basic Forms of Prophetic Speech*, London, 1967, pp. 112 ff.

in K. Koch's explanation of the continuing interest of Israelite sagas for later generations of Israelites.[32] Here, it is to be noted, there is no explicit reference to Lévy-Bruhl, but only to Wheeler Robinson, and Koch's use of corporate personality is a good example of the way in which the theory has become part of the stock in trade of some Old Testament scholars. In his article 'The Hebrew Conception of Corporate Personality'[33] Wheeler Robinson rightly drew attention to that aspect of English legal practice (from which the term 'corporate personality' was taken) in which corporations aggregate are regarded as greater than the sum of the life of the individuals who presently compose them, so that a corporation aggregate has a legal 'personality' which carries on from generation to generation. Wheeler Robinson compared this persistence of the legal 'personality' to the idea in the Old Testament that a man lives on in his own family, and that the family of Israel, or of a tribe or clan lives on in its members over the generations. It is probable, however, that Wheeler Robinson was not just drawing an analogy between corporations aggregate and Hebrew social groups. No doubt also the notion of extension of personality (which was involved in corporate representation) was in his mind when he wrote of social groups extending over the generations. In his use of corporate personality in describing Israelite saga, Koch implies that because of the way in which the personality of an individual not only extends into that of his social group, but also does this across the barriers of time, the Hebrew listener to a saga in Old Testament times could relate his own life much more directly to the hero of the saga, and to its events, than would be true for a modern reader. Thus 'saga has a different effectiveness from that of historical writing, bridging the gap between the present and the past, and showing that what appears as past events contains a hidden relevance to the present. The narrator and his hearers identify themselves with the deeds and sufferings of their forebears. God's intervention in favour of their forebears is intervention in favour of themselves. . . . Hence the Israelite can relate his own life to that of the hero, because the conception of

[32] K. Koch, *Was ist Formgeschichte?*, Neukirchen-Vluyn, 1964, pp. 176 ff., 1974³, pp. 188 ff. E.T. *The Growth of the Biblical Tradition*, London, 1969, pp. 153 ff.
[33] H. W. Robinson in *Werden und Wesen des Alten Testaments, BZAW* 66, 1936, pp. 49–62.

"corporate personality" is natural to him.'[34] Here again, we have something which is impossible to prove, except that we can say that if the position depends on the idea of extension of personality, then it is based ultimately upon Lévy-Bruhl's law of participation, which is unacceptable, anthropologically speaking. There might, of course, be other reasons for maintaining, with Koch, that processes of perception and appropriation not available to moderns, came into play when ancient Hebrew sagas were recounted, but these would need to be explained and justified.

It is difficult to escape the conclusion that scholars who have applied to the Old Testament the theories of Lévy-Bruhl, whether at first or second hand, have had little awareness of the theoretical presuppositions of his position. For all that Lévy-Bruhl did not practise what he preached, he nevertheless believed that he was giving a proper explanation of the evidence about primitives that was available to him. Had Old Testament students realized more fully that in theory his position implied that the way of thinking of primitives could only be understood in terms of all the social factors that moulded their lives, and had they therefore sought to interpret Hebrew thought in terms of the evidence of the Old Testament taken as a whole, it is doubtful whether they would have read theories of primitive mentality into parts of the Old Testament evidence. As mentioned earlier, Lévy-Bruhl's general theoretical position is still tenable, and to this extent he may give a lead for future Old Testament work.[35]

The third and final attempt to explain the information about the lives of primitives which we shall consider, is that of the philosopher and historian of science, Ernst Cassirer. Cassirer stood in the stream of philosophy influenced by the work of Immanuel Kant

[34] Koch, *Was ist Formgeschichte?*, p. 176 and n. 25, 3rd ed., p. 191, n. 28. E.T., p. 156 and n. 26.

[35] A refinement of Lévy-Bruhl's position is to be found in W. F. Albright's *History, Archaeology and Christian Humanism*, London, 1965, pp. 66 ff. (There are also references to Albright's earlier work on this subject.) Albright seems to accept that all human thinking has developed through the same stages, but he posits a third stage in between logical mentality and pre-logical mentality, namely, empirico-logical thinking. This allows for Lévy-Bruhl's posthumously published denial of some of his earlier views, based on the recognition that in fact in many areas of life, primitives think quite normally. However, there is no evidence that Albright is familiar with anthropological objections to Lévy-Bruhl's theories.

EA

(1724–1804), and he attempted to explain the data about primitives in terms of Kantian epistemology. Kant had argued that in perception, the sense impressions that came in on a person from outside were not received by a blank and passive mind. Rather, the mind played an active part in encountering the sense impressions, and in imposing upon them the *a priori* forms of space, time and number. Whereas Kant held that his account of the *a priori* forms held true for all human perception, Cassirer attempted to define what the *a priori* forms must be like for primitives, whose thought was not the empirical consciousness of modern man, but what Cassirer called mythopoeic thought.[36]

In mythopoeic thought, sense impressions were not broken down into small units and then re-synthesized in terms of previously perceived objects; i.e. mythopoeic thought was not analytic. Rather, the quality of sense impressions rather than their quantity was experienced, and things were perceived as 'wholes.' For example, whereas in empirical consciousness a book with yellow covers would be perceived as consisting of paper, print, white colour, black colour, yellow colour, and so on, in mythopoeic thought, these individual ingredients would not be clearly distinguished. Moreover, the yellowness of a book would be perceived as an outstanding quality of the object, and if another object, not a book, were perceived, which was also yellow, mythopoeic thought would presume that there was a connection between the two things in virtue of their yellowness. In turn, this would affect the practice of magic; for by affecting one object, one would also be affecting the whole class of objects which, for example, had yellowness as a quality. The mythopoeic form of space was concerned with the fact that certain areas were believed to be sacred, and were thus marked off from other space. Thus, their distinctive quality was perceived. Similarly, the quality of certain events at certain times of the year was the hallmark of the mythopoeic consciousness of time, so that it was dominated by the rhythm of recurring seasons of the year, and notable events associated with them. Number was a quality which bound together classes of objects which shared the same number.

Some of Cassirer's position, as outlined above, will immediately

---

[36] E. Cassirer, *Die Philosophie der Symbolischen Formen II. Das Mythische Denken*, Berlin, 1925. E.T., *The Philosophy of Symbolic Forms 2. Mythical Thought*, New Haven, 1955.

remind the reader of Frazer's views of the causality ot magic. But Cassirer himself was clear that his position differed from those of both Frazer and Lévy-Bruhl.[37] Frazer, according to Cassirer, had made magic have far too much in common with science. He had supposed that the same mental processes were at work, whether a primitive were working magic, or a scientist was conducting an experiment. They differed simply according to the laws by which they worked; scientific laws for the scientist, and the laws of contagion and similarity for the primitive practising magic. On the other hand, Lévy-Bruhl had over-exaggerated the difference between primitive and modern mentality. Cassirer wished to maintain that the mental processes of primitives and moderns were basically the same, and that there was a logic about the former, although that logic was not to be understood in terms of empirical consciousness. By reconstructing the *a priori* forms of perception in mythopoeic thought, Cassirer hoped to explain the oddity of primitive thought to the modern mind, while pointing to the consistency of primitive thought within its own terms. Further, Cassirer did not believe that mythopoeic thought inevitably gave way to empirical consciousness. The two could to some extent exist alongside each other, and mythopoeic thought had provided much of the artistic and religious symbolism of mankind. Empirical consciousness had not made an appearance until the Greeks began to make abstract hypotheses about the world, and to test and modify these hypotheses. Therefore, the ancient Hebrews and their civilized neighbours in the ancient world thought not in terms of empirical consciousness, but according to the forms of mythopoeic thought.

The criticisms that can be brought against Cassirer are similar to those brought against Frazer and Lévy-Bruhl, namely, that he is attempting to describe largely pre-fieldwork information about primitives, and that therefore he can make no allowance for the symbolic or non-causative understanding of magic on the part of many primitives. Also, it is arguable that had Cassirer not written *The Philosophy of Symbolic Forms* at a time when many Babylonian texts were being interpreted in a magical way, he might have recognized that many aspects of ancient Near Eastern thought were indeed appropriate to empirical consciousness. Cassirer's position

[37] For Cassirer's critique of Frazer and Lévy-Bruhl see *The Myth of the State*, New Haven, 1946, pp. 8 ff.

has come to be used in Old Testament study largely by way of the symposium, *Before Philosophy*, edited by H. and H. A. Frankfort.[38] The book is a symposium, and it must be stressed that the contributors do not necessarily, therefore, start from identical presuppositions. The opening essay, by the editors, is entitled 'Myth and Reality,' and a concluding chapter by the same authors has the title 'The Emancipation of Thought from Myth.' Although these chapters contain no explicit evidence of dependence on Cassirer (Vol. 2 of *The Philosophy of Symbolic Forms* is, however, mentioned as 'suggested reading' at the end of the chapter 'Myth and Reality') it is clear that at some points, Cassirer is the basis of the Frankforts' position.[39] For example, the *a priori* forms of space and time (called 'concepts') are discussed, and brief quotations will indicate the similarity of the position to that of Cassirer. Of space, the Frankforts say

> The spatial concepts of the primitive are concrete orientations; they refer to localities which have an emotional colour; they may be familiar or alien, hostile or friendly. Beyond the scope of mere individual experience the community is aware of certain cosmic events which invest regions of space with a particular significance. . . . Thus mythopoeic thought may succeed no less than modern thought in establishing a co-ordinated spatial system; but the system is determined, not by objective measurements, but by an emotional recognition of values.[40]

And on time, we may quote

> The mythopoeic conception of time is, like that of space, qualitative and concrete, not quantitative and abstract. Mythopoeic thought does not know time as a uniform duration or as a succession of qualitatively indifferent moments.[41]

The continuation of this passage, indeed, has a reference to Cassirer, though only by way of illustration of the point, and not

---

[38] H. Frankfort and others, *Before Philosophy*, Harmondsworth, 1949; American edition, *The Intellectual Adventure of Ancient Man*, Chicago, 1946. The British edition lacks the essay by W. A. Irwin on Ancient Israel.
[39] The dependence of the Frankforts on Cassirer is asserted by P. Radin, *Primitive Man as Philosopher*, New York, 1957 (Rev. Ed.), p. xxvi.
[40] *Before Philosophy*, p. 30.   [41] Op. cit., p. 33.

to state dependence on him. Statements about causality in primitive thought stress, as does Cassirer, both the inner logic of the causal process as well as its difference from a modern viewpoint.[42] It can confidently be asserted that whatever criticisms can be brought against Cassirer apply with equal force to the exposition of mythopoeic thought in *Before Philosophy*.

The Old Testament is also discussed in the essays by the Frankforts, but in this case, there is a tendency to isolate ancient Hebrew thought from that of Israel's neighbours.[43] This is done by arguing that the Hebrews attained to such a transcendent view of God, that the abstract thought involved lifted them above mythopoeic thought. It is this aspect of the writings of the Frankforts, the stressing of the uniqueness of ancient Israel in opposition to her neighbours, which has attracted Old Testament scholars such as G. E. Wright. Wright's book, *The Old Testament Against its Environment* confessedly follows the Frankforts in arguing for the uniqueness of the faith of Israel in the ancient Near East.[44] However, it is arguable that in appealing to distinctive religious beliefs as the distinguishing marks of the ancient Israelites, the Frankforts and Wright are not only going beyond Cassirer, who certainly regarded the Hebrew belief in God as part of mythopoeic thought, but they are also confusing theology with epistemology. One has no wish to deny the uniqueness of the faith of Israel; but in interpreting the Old Testament in the light of the ancient Near East, scholars should be aware, if at all possible, of the anthropological assumptions of their interpretation. Interpretations based ultimately on Cassirer certainly need re-examination.

This chapter has been mainly negative, and indeed it has little to offer in conclusion by way of positive thoughts. This will be in line with what was said in the opening chapter, when it was remarked that in some cases, the contribution of modern social anthropology to Old Testament study would be mainly negative. But it is also in line, I believe, with the fact that recent anthropological discussion of the possible differences in modes of thought between societies has become aware of how little, in fact, is still known about how one is to frame the relevant questions, let alone answer them.

[42] Op. cit., pp. 27 ff.   [43] Op. cit., pp. 241 ff.
[44] G. E. Wright, *The Old Testament Against its Environment*, London, 1950. See the index entry under Frankfort, H.

In the conclusion to their Introduction to *Modes of Thought*, the editors confess that

> perhaps the only definite conclusion that can be drawn from the discussions in this volume is that the essays have, in a number of ways, made it even clearer to us where we must doubt and where we must enquire further. . . . Yet this very lack of definite conclusion or of verified hypothesis is in itself a significant feature of the volume.[45]

Among the important points made by the contributors the following are noteworthy.

First, it is argued that there has been a circularity in supposing that peoples classified as scientific or primitive on the basis of material culture, must also think differently. It may be that they do, but this should not be assumed; and if peoples were to be classified by means other than their material culture, say, on the basis of aspects of their language, results might be very different. There is the danger that in trying to find differences in modes of thought between peoples who have been classified on the basis of *material* culture, differences in thought will be exaggerated. Second, insufficient attention has been paid to the question of what constitutes a *basic* difference in thought between peoples. Once this problem is faced, the further question arises whether it would be possible to distinguish societies on the grounds that some possessed basic differences of thought that were not to be found elsewhere. If these questions could be answered, they would generate an enormous amount of research.

Third, the point is made several times in *Modes of Thought* that it will not be possible to understand how other societies think unless we understand how our own society thinks.[46] To take one problem, Sybil Wolfram asks the question, what does it mean to say that our society is characterized by scientific thinking ?

> Is it that there should be a body of knowledge which can in some sense be said to belong to the society, as we may be said to

---

[45] *Modes of Thought*, p. 62.

[46] Cp. my comment in *J.T.S.* XXI, 1970, p. 13, about the use in Old Testament study of 'unexamined generalizations about Hebrew thought and Western thought.'

have a body of knowledge about the natural world although many of us do not have it ? Or is it rather that the society should conduct its affairs on a scientific basis, or that its members on the whole think in a scientific manner, or merely that they have a penchant for 'scientific' support for beliefs they may hold, as others perhaps appeal to tradition ?[47]

These rhetorical questions lead to a fourth point which is that often in the comparison of primitive and modern thought, like has not been compared with like. The observed behaviour of primitives has not been compared with the observed behaviour of moderns; rather, it has been compared with an idealized and often unexamined view of 'modern scientific thought.'

Clearly, much remains to be done in work on modes of thought, and for the time being Old Testament scholars may have to content themselves with being cautious when they make pronouncements about Hebrew mentality. They will need to follow with interest the continuing discussion among anthropologists about the understanding and interpretation of the thought of peoples separated by culture and by history from modern Western culture.

[47] *Modes of Thought*, pp. 357–8.

4

Folklore[1]

Folklore is no longer a branch of anthropology, and one eminent folklorist has recently complained about the lack of liaison between the two disciplines.[2] However, anthropology and folklore have many areas of common interest, as indicated by the fact that Dorson's *The British Folklorists* devotes a good deal of space to men such as Tylor, Frazer, and Lang. In Old Testament study, theories by folklorists about traditions transmitted orally have been used by Old Testament scholars, in the way that anthropological theories have been used, and this is why a chapter on folklore is included at this point.

Although the word 'folk-lore' (with a hyphen) was coined by the British antiquary William John Thoms in 1846,[3] the study of the traditions, beliefs and customs of the common people goes back a good deal farther. Once again, our survey begins in Germany; for if Thomas Croker's volume *Fairy Legends and Traditions of the South of Ireland* published in 1825 was 'the first intentional field collection to be made in Britain,'[4] it was nevertheless several years later than the famous collection entitled *Kinder- und Hausmärchen* by the brothers Jacob and Wilhelm Grimm. Of this latter work, the first volume appeared in 1812, the second in 1815, and a

---

[1] The *Oxford English Dictionary* defines Folk-lore as 'The traditional beliefs, legends, and customs, current among the common people; the study of these.' The supplement to the *O.E.D.*, Vol. I, 1972, notes that the word is not now hyphenated.

[2] See below, n. 47.

[3] Richard M. Dorson, *The British Folklorists*, London, 1968, p. 1.

[4] Op. cit., p. 45.

second edition appeared already in 1819.[5] The Grimms were not without their forerunners in Germany either. In 1782–1787 J. K. A. Musäus published a five-volume collection of German folktales,[6] and the influence of Herder was, of course, considerable.[7] But in many ways, the Grimms were pioneers, and it is no accident that it is their work above all that has become the foundation for subsequent research. Their influence on Old Testament study was by way of their Göttingen colleague, the orientalist Heinrich Ewald, and two aspects of their work were important here. First, their definitions of types of folk tradition, and second, their interest in oral transmission.

The Grimms believed that myth was the basic form of folk tradition, and by myth they understood belief in gods, and by myths, stories about gods.[8] It is not so easy to understand their definition of another main form of tradition, saga. They seem to have regarded saga as an expression, often with supernatural elements derived from the mythical substratum, of popular beliefs and fears. Yet sagas were also bound up intrinsically with history in the pre-literary periods of a people's life. For example, an historical event could occur and leave its mark on human memory; then, as the event was related by word of mouth, the processes of oral transmission would shape the event into saga. It would be invested with the supernatural, and it would take on a new appearance. Saga was not necessarily unhistorical or anti-historical, neither was it what today would be regarded as accurate history. It might or might not have a basis in history, but whatever the case in this latter regard, it would be an expression of popular beliefs and fears. On the other hand, folktales (German *Märchen*) had as their primary purpose the amusement and entertainment of their hearers. In all their work, the Grimms paid special attention to the place of oral transmission in the formation of folk traditions.[9]

Ewald, whose *Geschichte des Volkes Israel* was published from

---

[5] See the edition of the *Kinder- und Hausmärchen* published in 1971 by the *Wissenschaftliche Buchgesellschaft*, Darmstadt. For a recent English translation see F. P. Magoun and A. H. Krappe, *German Folk Tales*, S. Illinois Univ. Press, 1960.

[6] See L. Denecke, *Jacob Grimm und sein Bruder Wilhelm*, Stuttgart, 1971, p. 64.

[7] Op. cit., p. 64.

[8] A. Jolles, *Einfache Formen*, Stuttgart, 1968[4], p. 94.

[9] Denecke, op. cit., p. 73.

1843 onwards,[10] was influenced by the Grimms' definition of myth and saga, and by their interest in oral transmission. He accepted the view that myths were stories about gods derived from belief in gods, and he concluded that because the Old Testament was predominantly monotheistic, it contained only a few remnants of myths. This view was in sharp contrast to the opinion of scholars of the end of the previous century, and of the early nineteenth century who, understanding myth in a different sense from Ewald, used this concept positively and extensively in their interpretation of the Old Testament.[11]

Ewald's most important work, however, was in connection with saga. He tended to ignore that part of the Grimms' thesis which was concerned with the influence of the mythical substratum on the form of saga; his main concern was with historical reconstruction. Thus, he concentrated on the part played by memory in the recollection of historical events, and how memory preserved such recollections and formed them into greater units. He maintained that newer recollections tended to oust older memories, so that the more the tradition preserved about a particular person, the more likely it was that he was a fresher figure in the memory.[12] Against this, one had to allow that prominent figures like David or Moses could attract to themselves traditions of events which originally had no connection with them. Another feature of the tradition was that it tended to heighten the supernatural element in a recollection, the longer the period of transmission. Ewald recognized that annual ceremonies such as Passover were an aid to memory, as were stones and monuments that might be set up. He also pointed out that in the course of transmission, recollections of events could assume a stereotyped or rounded form, characterized by stereotyped details such as significant numbers of sons and daughters born to famous people.

[10] H. Ewald, *Geschichte des Volkes Israel*, Göttingen, 1843¹, E.T., London, 1867–86.   [11] See *Myth in Old Testament Interpretation*, Ch. 2.
[12] Note the use of exactly the same principle by M. Noth, *Überlieferungsgeschichte des Pentateuchs*, Stuttgart, 1948, pp. 113–14; E.T., *A History of Pentateuchal Tradition*, Englewood Cliffs, N.J., 1972, p. 103; and K. Koch, *Was ist Formgeschichte?*, 1964, p. 140, (3rd German ed., p. 154), E.T., *The Growth of the Biblical Tradition*, p. 126. In both cases Isaac is said to be historically prior to Abraham, because less is known about him. Koch states, 'The general rule in the transmission of the saga is that the least known figure is the original' (p. 126).

Ewald's careful examination of those traditions of the Old
Testament that could have been influenced by folklore processes
remained, as far as I know, the major attempt along these lines
until the work of scholars such as Gunkel and Frazer in the present
century. Gunkel's purpose was different from Ewald's. The latter
was concerned with the study of saga and oral transmission for the
purposes of reconstructing history. Gunkel did not exactly have an
aversion to history; but he considered it to be only one of the ways
in which religious truth could be conveyed or expressed. He was
much more interested in poetry, and he saw in folk tradition the
natural poetry of the people. His aim in comparing the Old
Testament with folk tradition was to recover the folk poetry of the
ancient Hebrew people, although he recognized that the beliefs
implied in such traditions were often incompatible with Yahwism
in its strictest form. Frazer, again, had a different purpose, which
will be mentioned after the outline of Gunkel's approach.

By way of introduction to Gunkel's work, it will not be without
anthropological interest to mention that although Gunkel began by
accepting the classifications of the brothers Grimm, he later partly
rejected their approach in favour of that advocated in Wilhelm
Wundt's *Völkerpsychologie*.[13] Briefly, Wundt maintained that it
was not myth that was the basic form of folk tradition, but folktale
(*Märchen*). In his view, mythologies only developed among more
settled and civilized people, whereas at a more primitive stage (as
evidenced by primitives of today) such belief in gods was not to be
found.[14] Readers will note the anthropological presupposition here:
the least technologically advanced primitives known to modern
man are our best guide for discovering primitive or earliest belief;
therefore whatever characterizes their life must be the most
primitive form. Gunkel's fullest expression of these later
(Wundtian) views was published in a small book in 1917, in
which he made a comparison between Old Testament traditions
and folktale (*Märchen*) traditions, from many parts of the world.[15]

For the purposes of the present chapter Gunkel's work will be
described under two headings: first, his detection in the Old
Testament of the *beliefs* associated with folktales; and secondly his

[13] W. Wundt, *Völkerpsychologie*, II Mythus und Religion, Leipzig,
1909.
[14] Cp. op. cit., part VI, book 3, pp. 131 ff., 1923³.
[15] H. Gunkel, *Das Märchen im Alten Testament*, Tübingen, 1917.

detection in the Old Testament of characteristic *motifs* of folk-tales. Gunkel's account of the beliefs associated with folktales, beliefs characteristic, according to Wundt's theory, of primitive peoples, is roughly as follows. The primitive tends to ascribe personality to the forces of nature, and especially to animals and plants. Thus, folktales arise in which animals and plants behave as human beings would behave; a particular animal (e.g. the lion) will be king of the animals, a particular plant (e.g. a mighty tree) king of the plants. The personification of the world of nature further requires that animals and plants can speak, and animals or birds often have better access to the divine than humans. Insofar as the *content* of folktales themselves expresses a 'religion,' it is not a religion centred on gods, but on giants, demons, ghosts, goblins, and the like. The 'religion' of folktales also involves magic.

Bearing these points in mind, it is possible to find in the Old Testament, beneath its monotheistic top layer, numerous examples of both the primitive mentality on which folktales are based, and the peculiar 'religion' which folktales express. In Judges 9:8–15 and II Kings 14:9 occur the two famous 'nature fables' of the Old Testament, in which plants speak to each other. Such fables must originate, according to Gunkel, from folktales in which animals and plants are regarded as persons, and the same explanation will serve for speaking animals in the Old Testament, such as Balaam's ass (Num. 22:28 ff.) and the serpent in the garden of Eden (Gen. 3:1 ff.). Balaam's ass is also a good example of the superior access to the divine enjoyed by animals over men (Num. 22:23 ff.). Other remnants of the 'personification' of nature are to be found in Leviathan (Job 40:25 Heb., 41:1 EVV) and Behemoth (Job 40:15 ff.) both of whom are 'kings' of the animals and Isa. 14:8, where the cypresses and cedars of Lebanon speak.[16]

Evidence of the 'religion' contained in folktales can be found in various references to giants (e.g. Gen. 6:4 ff.), to demons such as that with which Jacob wrestled (Gen. 32:23 ff.), or to the mys-terious three men who visited Abraham (Gen. 18:2 ff.). Magic featured often in Old Testament narratives. Elijah's mantle has power to work miracles after his death (II Kings 2:13–14) as does the corpse of Elisha (II Kings 13:20–1). The staves of Moses (Exodus 4:3 ff.), Aaron (Ex. 7:10 ff.) and Elisha (II Kings 4:29)

[16] See op. cit., pp. 20 ff., for further examples.

are believed to have supernatural powers; Moses (Ex. 15:25) and Elisha (II Kings 2:19) make bitter waters sweet, Elijah causes a jar of meal and a cruse of oil fat never to be exhausted, Joshua (Jos. 10:12 ff.) commands the sun to stand still, and requests by Gideon (Judges 6:36 ff.) that a fleece should be either dry or wet when the ground is the opposite, are granted.

In illustration of the thesis that typical folktale *motifs* were to be found in the Old Testament, Gunkel brought the following examples. The motif of the exposure of children underlies the story of Moses (Ex. 2:1–10) and possibly the passage of Ezekiel 16:1–14 where the history of Jerusalem is described in terms of the rescue of an abandoned maiden. This latter passage may also be an example of the motif of the poor, beautiful girl who becomes queen. The motif of the poor lad, or the younger brother, who becomes prince or ruler can be detected in the stories of Saul, Joseph, and David. David and Gideon are also younger brothers, and Joseph is an example of the motif in which the youngest brother[17] eventually delivers his eldest brothers and parents. The motif of the young person in opposition to his elders occurs in the stories about Jacob and Laban (Gen. 29–31), Samuel and the sons of Eli (I Sam. 3) and David and Saul (I Sam. 16 ff.).

The examples quoted represent only a sample of Gunkel's references, but I have tried to select them in order to indicate both the strengths and weaknesses of his position. The weaknesses will be most obviously apparent to the reader, who will rightly want to know whether Gunkel is suggesting that figures like Saul or David or various incidents in their lives are unhistorical, because they reflect typical motifs of folktales. In reply, it can be said that Gunkel was usually better at making comparisons than drawing out the implications of such comparisons, and that his use of folktales to illustrate Old Testament traditions sometimes went too far in the direction of historical scepticism.[18] One can also criticize Gunkel for a certain woodenness in his handling of Old Testament poetry. Must we really accept that any use of personification of the forces of nature in the poetry of prophetic books

[17] Joseph is in fact not the youngest brother, but is the youngest who is in a position to do anything.

[18] See the criticisms by O. Eissfeldt in 'Die Bedeutung der Märchenforschung für die Religionswissenschaft besonders für die Wissenschaft vom Alten Testament' in *Kleine Schriften*, I, Tübingen, 1962, pp. 23–32.

is a survival from folktales and the mentality which allegedly
produces them ?

On the other hand, we must not be blind to what Gunkel
achieved positively. He was undoubtedly correct in maintaining
that those Old Testament traditions that had been orally transmitted over a long period of time could have been affected by
folktale motifs, and he was correct to look for examples of such
motifs. Further, as mentioned above, Gunkel's broad understanding of what was meant by the 'truth' of the Old Testament
enabled him to see that accurate historical records were only one
way of conveying truth. Truth, in the sense of what the people had
come to know and believe about God, could also be expressed
with the help of folktale motifs, and in turn, these could assist
traditions about historical events to express an interpretation of the
events as the revelation of divine activity. Of course, Gunkel
wanted to go further than this, and to prove that the history of
Israelite religion was a history which involved the gradual victory
of Yahwism over the sort of mentality and religion presupposed
by folktales; but this former insight was nevertheless a valuable one.

Frazer's contribution to the discussion can be mentioned briefly.
His three-volume *Folk-Lore in the Old Testament* appeared at
about the same time as Gunkel's *Das Märchen im Alten Testament*,[19] but it had rather a different scope from Gunkel's book. In
his preface, Frazer explained that 'the scope of my work has
obliged me to dwell chiefly on the lower side of ancient Hebrew
life revealed in the Old Testament, on the traces of savagery and
superstition which are to be found in its pages . . . the revelation
of the baser elements which underlay the civilization of ancient
Israel . . . serves rather as a foil to enhance by contrast the glory
of a people which, from such dark depths of ignorance and cruelty,
could rise to such bright heights of wisdom and virtue.'[20] It will
be seen that Frazer was in agreement with Gunkel that comparative
folklore studies could discover a 'primitive' residuum in the Old
Testament. But whereas Gunkel's book was devoted to the
analysis and classification of Old Testament narratives in the light
of comparative folklore, Frazer's book was primarily *illustrative*.
It provided a mass of examples, taken from all over the world, of
narratives that displayed certain similarities with elements in Old

[19] J. G. Frazer, *Folk-Lore in the Old Testament*, London, 1918.
[20] Op. cit., Vol. I, p. x.

Testament narratives, and of course, it had all the strengths and weaknesses of Frazer's work. On the one hand, it was a monument of industry and eloquence; on the other hand, the illustrative material was of varying reliability, and the whole work was put together with little regard for differences of culture and time. The book remains a quarry of information to be used with care, and its influence has not been negligible even in recent Old Testament studies. Further, it has recently taken on a new lease of life in a one-volume up-dated edition by T. H. Gaster.[21]

A quite different book, first published in 1930 must be noted next. It is André Jolles's work *Einfache Formen* (Simple Forms), a difficult book, but one which has influenced both folklore and Old Testament studies.[22] One of the main concerns of the book is to account for the origin of the so-called simple forms that underlie the art forms of more developed literature; or perhaps a slightly different example will clarify the matter. If it is true that folktales have certain definite forms, e.g. that they often begin with the formula 'once upon a time' and end with the heroes living happily ever after, the question arises as to the origin of such forms. Clearly, once a form becomes established, people will adopt it deliberately; but how does a form originate and become established ? Jolles's explanation is not easy to understand; he seems to say that in certain social circles or circumstances, language creates simple forms in order to express what needs to be expressed. The forms are not consciously invented by anyone. They happen; and they happen because language needs them if it is to express the concerns of the particular circles or circumstances.

The part of Jolles's book that has most influenced Old Testament studies is that dealing with saga (German *Sage*), and it would be well to begin by mentioning that Jolles emphasizes the ambiguity of the word saga.[23] Jolles argues that the definitions of saga given in the *Oxford English Dictionary* are more satisfactory than many German attempts to define the word. The Oxford definition distinguishes between 'correct' and 'incorrect' uses of

---

[21] T. H. Gaster, *Myth, Legend and Custom in the Old Testament*, London, 1969.

[22] A. Jolles, *Einfache Formen*, Tübingen, 1930, 1968[4]; see also K. Ranke (ed.), *Internationaler Kongress der Volkserzählungsforscher in Kiel und Kopenhagen*, Berlin, 1961, pp. 1–11.

[23] Jolles, op. cit., pp. 62 ff.

the word. The primary 'correct' meaning is 'any of the narrative compositions in prose that were written in Iceland or Norway during the middle ages.' This meaning can then be extended to cover 'a narrative having the (real or supposed) characteristics of the Icelandic sagas.' Under 'incorrect' uses, the Oxford definition indicates 'a story, popularly believed to be a matter of fact, which has been developed by gradual accretions in the course of ages, and has been handed down by oral tradition; historical or heroic legend, as distinguished both from authentic history and from intentional fiction.' Jolles fastens onto the primary 'correct' use, that connecting it with medieval prose compositions from Iceland or Norway, and argues that as a 'simple form' saga originates in the type of family that has a history which extends over a number of generations and which is described in such prose compositions. The family is closely knit, and its own concerns are so important to it, that the affairs of the family become the affairs in effect of the whole world in which the family lives. Saga in this sense is the spontaneous creation of language within the setting of such a family. It is a 'simple form' created by the necessity to express and narrate its concerns. Interestingly for English readers, Jolles regards the use of the word saga by Galsworthy in his famous *Forsyte Saga* not as an example of 'incorrect' usage, but as an example of the adoption in literature of an original 'simple form.' The *Forsyte Saga* is saga in that it relates the history and concerns of a family.

In an attempt to illustrate his point more clearly, Jolles makes a number of comparisons between narratives about families which are and are not saga as he understands the word. One comparison involves Old Testament examples.[24] Jolles considers that the patriarchal narratives are saga, because they are about a family which extends for several generations, and which seems to occupy almost the whole of the world stage in its outlook. On the other hand, the narratives about the family of David in II Samuel and I Kings are not sagas. Although the latter are indeed narratives about a family, their aim is not to relate matters of concern to the family, but matters of concern to the state of ancient Israel.

At this point, we need to evaluate Jolles's position as a whole. It is, of course, impossible to understand it fully except in the

[24] Jolles, op. cit., pp. 87–8.

context of German romanticism and idealism. This is why Jolles's book, with its appeal to the idea of language expressing itself in different 'simple forms' will be strange for many British readers. Further, if the British empirical tradition finds this sort of thing vague, it must also be said that recently in some quarters in Germany, there has been a desire (as will be spelt out later) to make Jolles's sort of approach more acceptable by replacing with a psychological explanation the notion of the language expressing itself in certain 'simple forms.'[25] It should also be pointed out that it is unfortunate that Jolles has allowed the Oxford Dictionary to get away with the notion of 'correct' and 'incorrect' uses of the word saga. It would be much less question-begging to distinguish between 'narrower' and 'broader' definitions, and to note that the 'broader' definition of the English word saga (i.e. the Oxford Dictionary's 'incorrect' use) corresponds closely to the German word *Sage*, especially as applied to Old Testament material by Ewald.

Criticisms apart, however, Jolles's book has posed questions that need to be faced, and it has suggested further lines of enquiry, as will be noted later. For the moment, it is necessary to see how he has influenced Old Testament studies. Two scholars in particular, C. Westermann and K. Koch, have taken up Jolles's position. Westermann[26] has accepted Jolles's classification of the patriarchal narratives, and has argued that they can only be properly understood when they are recognized to be the product of a particular type of family life. The contents of the patriarchal narratives are not therefore to be combed so that history can be produced; the contents must be seen to be the expression of the concerns of a family: a man (Abraham) wants a son; his wife (Sarah) is in danger; brothers (Jacob and Esau) are in opposition, and so on. It must be said that Westermann's exposition is a satisfying one, and one which enables the debate over the historicity of the patriarchal narratives to be seen in better perspective. I am not altogether happy, however, with the way in which Westermann accepts Jolles, apparently without a consideration of the basic position which the particular thesis implies. Does Westermann accept Jolles's theories about the origin of 'simple forms' like saga in

[25] K. Ranke, loc. cit.

[26] C. Westermann, 'Arten der Erzählung in der Genesis,' in *Forschung am Alten Testament*, Munich, 1964, pp. 9–91.

FA

terms of a necessary expression of language ? Is it safe to argue directly, as Jolles himself has done, from Icelandic families of c. A.D. 1100–1200 or later, to a Semitic family of about 1700 B.C. ? While finding Westermann's exposition suggestive, I cannot help also regarding it as another example of how Old Testament scholarship can take over the results of studies in a different discipline without evaluating the presuppositions of these results. That Westermann is inclined to do this sort of thing is amply illustrated from the treatment of the Flood narratives in his Genesis commentary.[27] Because he wishes to prove that all flood stories are originally connected with rituals, and that therefore the flood narratives of the ancient Near East must also have been originally connected with ritual, he uses examples taken from Frazer's *Folk-Lore in the Old Testament* to furnish evidence for the original connection between flood stories and rituals in the ancient Near East. Readers will at once notice the anthropological presupposition that what can be demonstrated for primitives must therefore once have been true for earliest man. Further, not only does Westermann use Frazer without being aware of the difficulties inherent in Frazer's material and methodology, he also seems to ignore Frazer's warnings that some of the flood stories found among primitives, even if attached to rituals, may have resulted from versions of the biblical account as taught by missionaries.

Klaus Koch's discussion of saga and legend in his book *The Growth of the Biblical Tradition* contains the only systematic treatment known to me in English translation which seriously considers the work of Jolles.[28] Before we consider what I regard as Koch's most helpful suggestions, it is necessary to point out one piece of methodological confusion in his discussion of saga. In our consideration of Jolles, we saw that in talking about saga as a simple form, Jolles accepted for his purposes the Oxford Dictionary's 'correct' definition of saga, and ignored its list of 'incorrect' uses. However, as argued above, it is question-begging to talk about 'correct' and 'incorrect' uses. We saw that one of the 'incorrect' uses of saga

---

[27] C. Westermann, *Genesis* (Biblischer Kommentar: Altes Testament), Neukirchen-Vluyn, 1966 ff., pp. 68–9.
[28] K. Koch, *The Growth of the Biblical Tradition*, pp. 148 ff. (1st German ed., pp. 167 ff., 3rd ed., 182 ff.)

was in the sense of heroic legend, and it has to be accepted that to many German speakers, *Sage* means primarily heroic saga or legend, i.e. stories about the exploits of great heroes.[29] Jolles had suggested that the heroic saga was part of the family saga, but later an opposing view was put forward that the family saga developed out of the heroic saga.[30] One wants to ask at this point whether it is in fact necessary to try to relate family and heroic saga together in this way. Is it not more likely that the term saga has been attached to two different types of narrative whose original relationship (if any) is not recoverable ? Koch, however, accepts that family and heroic saga are in fact related. He classifies the patriarchal narratives as family saga and the traditions about David and Saul as heroic saga. On the assumption of a relationship between the two he asserts that 'Israelite saga underwent quite considerable changes between the time of the nomadic patriarchs and their people and the start of the monarchical period when the tribes were permanently settled.'[31] However, there is no evidence for such development other than that Koch has labelled two types of narratives as saga, and has assumed a relationship between them which he then 'explains' in terms of development. It is doubtful whether one can use the classification and comparison of literary forms to reconstruct their history in this way.

Koch is more helpful, in my view, when he reasserts something already said by Gunkel, that narratives such as sagas enable people to express their hopes and fears, and their belief that God is at work in their history. As Koch well says

> Sagas are reality poeticized. As everyone knows, some of the greatest Old Testament books are poetic, such as the Psalter or the book of Job, for poetry can provide insights into the final truths of existence which are inaccessible to science. Therefore poetry plays a necessary part in any attempt to approach these

[29] Cp. Westermann, 'Arten der Erzählungen in der Genesis,' p. 39. 'In distinction from the Icelandic word *saga*, the German word *Sage* is traditionally connected with the heroic saga in such a way, that where German is spoken, the word *Sage* suggests, in the first instance, heroic saga' (translation mine). For the difference between the German *Legende* and the English 'legend,' see Koch, pp. 195 ff. (1st German ed., p. 209 ff., 3rd ed., pp. 239 ff.)

[30] Koch, op. cit., p. 151 (1st German ed., p. 171, 3rd ed., p. 186).

[31] Koch, op. cit., p. 152 (1st German ed., pp. 171-2, 3rd ed., p. 186).

final truths. . . . Why then should not the poetry of the people themselves be a medium for divine revelation ?[32]

And later, writing about sagas and legends (legends understood along the lines suggested by Jolles) he comments

> Both the legend and the saga are concerned with God's action on earth. Both look beyond the ordinary connection of earthly events *and show how God is at work within these events.* Historical writing was not able to do this, being concerned only with the human level of failure or success, and merely accepting the fact that God influenced this (see the transmission [*sic*] of David's succession to the throne, II Sam. ix ff.). However, sagas and legends are also concerned with *how* God influences events, the saga more with the external, objective story, and the legend more with the internal, subjective aspects of it. Thus both ways of thinking play an essential part in the biblical writings. Divine revelation and divine action should not only be expressed in the language of metaphysics, for this has no connection with history. Sagas and legends, therefore, do not conflict with the general link between faith and history, but on the contrary emphasize it.[33]

I would not want to accept everything in this passage; but I would draw special attention to the suggestion that because saga and legend are closer than history to metaphysics, they may indeed help historical narratives to express a metaphysical dimension perceived in history by faith. I shall return to this point later.

Before I turn to consider recent developments in folklore studies, the work of T. H. Gaster must be mentioned. Gaster has recently published an up-dated version of Frazer's *Folk-Lore in the Old Testament* under the title *Myth, Legend and Custom in the Old Testament*, although it must be stated that Gaster's aims are different from Frazer's. If Frazer stressed the similarities between folklore as found among primitives, and those parts of the Old Testament that still betray the earlier primitive thoughts and be-liefs of the Hebrew forebears, Gaster stresses that the folktale motifs of Old Testament traditions (in common with folktale motifs to be found in all literatures) express something of the experiences of men of all ages, including modern man. The Old

[32] Koch, op. cit., p. 156 (1st German ed., pp. 175–6, 3rd ed., p. 191).

[33] Op. cit., p. 199 (3rd German ed., p. 243). This passage does not appear in the 1st German edition.

Testament stories are, he writes 'paradigms of the continuing
human situation, we are involved in them ... we are all expelled
from our Edens and sacrifice our happiness to the ambitions of
our intellects. All of us metaphorically flee our Egypts, receive our
revelation, and trek through our deserts to a promised land which
only our children or our children's children may enjoy.'[34]

However, in many ways, Gaster's most satisfying work on the
presence of folktale motifs in the Old Testament is not in *Myth,
Legend and Custom*, but in his article some twenty years earlier in
Funk and Wagnall's *Standard Dictionary of Mythology, Folklore
and Legend*.[35] In his book, Gaster has had to follow the format
laid down by Frazer, which is to start at Genesis and to work
through to Malachi, adducing as he goes, parallels from world folk
literature. The difficulty of this approach is that it makes it difficult
for the reader to appreciate what *types* of folk motif there are in the
Old Testament, and how these compare with motifs in other
literature. The value of Gunkel's book was precisely that it tried
to classify elements in the narrative according to types and forms.
Of course, Gaster's book has the advantage that because it works
through the Old Testament text from beginning to end, it makes
it easier for the reader to find folklore parallels to any particular
part of the Old Testament on which he happens to be working.
But a good index could do the same in a book that worked primarily from the classification of form and types. A very important
feature of *Myth, Legend and Custom* is that, in it, Gaster constantly
relates motifs to be found in the Old Testament to motifs found
elsewhere, for example by reference to Thompson's *Motif-Index
of Folk Literature*,[36] and although the book has a short appendix
indicating which of Thompson's motifs are mentioned, my impression, from my use of both Gaster and Thompson, is that many
more parallels between Old Testament material and Thompson's
motifs exist than Gaster's index indicates.

The reason, then, why the earlier article entitled 'Semitic
Folklore' is perhaps more satisfying, is because it is not limited by
the need to work through the Old Testament text from Genesis to

---

[34] *Myth, Legend and Custom*, p. xxxiv.

[35] Funk and Wagnall's *Standard Dictionary of Mythology, Folklore
and Legend*, New York, 1949–50, article 'Semitic Folklore.'

[36] S. Thompson, *Motif-Index of Folk Literature*, 6 vols., Bloomington
(Enlarged Ed., second printing), 1966.

Malachi, but rather classifies the motifs to be found in the Old
Testament, comparing them with the standard motifs classified by
Thompson and others. Gaster finds that the biblical folktales
embrace almost all the usual categories: cosmogonic tales, animal
tales, tabu tales (Lot's wife; Miriam's leprosy), magic tales (Moses'
and Aaron's staffs, etc.), tales of marvellous creatures, tales of
deception (Leah as false bride), tales of rewards and punishments,
tales of sex (Judah and Tamar), and aetiological tales. Gaster
regards the source of this material as primarily the popular lore of
Canaan, although he allows that some stories go back to much
older originals. In the conclusions that he draws from his comparisons, it is arguable that he is less satisfactory. His opinion that
'the fundamentalist position that the stories are genuine history
becomes altogether untenable, when analogies and parallels are
found to exist throughout the world'[37] is unnecessarily sceptical
because it does not allow adequately for the interplay between oral
traditions about historical events, and folktale motifs, in the oral
transmission process. However, Gaster is surely right to argue
that 'the vast majority of biblical scholars have been slow to
appreciate the implications of a folkloristic approach.'[38] Such a
comment is all the more important in the light of recent developments in folklore studies, to which I now turn.

In his opening address to the 1959 International Congress of
Folklorists in Kiel and Copenhagen, the Göttingen scholar Kurt
Ranke discussed Jolles's theory of 'simple forms.'[39] Ranke paid
tribute to the work of Jolles, but stressed that it was impossible
for modern folklorists to accept Jolles's romantic theories about
the origin of simple forms (a point that does not seem to have
been appreciated by Old Testament users of Jolles, such as
Westermann and Koch).[40] However, according to Ranke, it might

[37] Article, 'Semitic Folklore,' pp. 986-7.
[38] Op. cit., p. 986. This criticism would not apply to W. Baumgartner.
See his article 'Israelitisch-Griechische Sagenbeziehungen' (1944),
reprinted in *Zum Alten Testament und seiner Umwelt*, Leiden, 1959.
Baumgartner compares motifs in Old Testament material with motifs
classified in A. Aarne, *Verzeichnis der Märchentypen*, Helsinki, 1910.
[39] K. Ranke, 'Einfache Formen,' in K. Ranke (ed.) *Internationaler
Kongress der Volkserzählungsforscher in Kiel und Kopenhagen*, pp. 1-11.
[40] Cp. also Linda Degh's reference to André Jolles's 'outdated ideas'
in her article 'The "Belief Legend" in Modern Society,' in *American Folk
Legend, A Symposium*, ed. W. D. Hand, Berkeley, Calif., 1971, p. 56.

be possible to substitute for Jolles's romantic view of the language expressing itself in simple forms, an explanation in terms of modern social psychology. In this latter connection Ranke stresses the need for inter-disciplinary co-operation between folklore studies, and fields such as anthropology and psychology. We recognize increasingly today, argues Ranke, that what a man is, is to some extent shaped by the community and the communal forces to which he is exposed. These forces include the history, beliefs, values, setting, and environment of the community of which he is a member. Simple forms may be the expression of the collective soul or spirit of the community, understanding the notions of collective soul or spirit as an interaction between man's basic needs and feelings as an individual and the shaping forces at work in his community. In this case, simple forms may arise as the expression of particular and different needs of man in community. For example, folktale (*Märchen*) could be seen as an expression of a desire for a higher order and justice in the world, especially on the part of the poor and oppressed. It would also express the human desire for luck, and an improvement in one's lot. In this way it could be seen why folktales so often were stories about the despised or outcast person (e.g. Cinderella) whose lot was dramatically improved. Saga, on the other hand (Ranke clearly has in mind heroic saga) would express something of the futility of life in a world where ultimately man could not withstand the cosmic forces which brought tragedy and ruin to the innocent.

On the subject of folktale motifs, although Ranke regards these as important, he stresses that the same motif can be expressed differently depending on the sort of simple form in which it appears. For example, the Jephthah story in Judges 11 contains the motif of a vow of a warrior which ultimately leads to the sacrifice of his only daughter. In a folktale, this motif would be so expressed that the story ended happily, with love overcoming the difficulties. As a saga, however (heroic saga), it would end in tragedy, with the human participants unable to overrule the inevitable cruel outcome of the drama.[41]

Ranke has not been without his critics. In a paper presented to

[41] For similar type or form studies of folktale and saga, see M. Lüthi, *Volksmärchen und Volkssage. Zwei Grundformen erzählender Dichtung*, Bern und München, 1961.

the same International Congress, Kurt Scheier argued that it was
not as easy to separate the simple forms as Ranke supposed; nor
was it so easy to itemize the particular psychological 'need' which
each form allegedly expressed.[42] However, if Scheier disagreed
with Ranke over the possibility of neatly classifying simple forms
and what they expressed, he was at one with Ranke in stressing
the need for a social psychological approach to the *function* of folk
traditions. We must accept as axiomatic, Scheier argues, that a
folk tradition expresses a basic human need, and goes far beyond
the purpose of merely conveying information. Further, Scheier is
of the opinion that although new cultural conditions may lead to
the decline of certain folktale forms, they also lead to the creation
of new forms through which man's hopes and aspirations are
expressed; and this is as true of the twentieth century as it is of
any other century.

Ranke and Scheier are not alone in adopting a sort of Jungian
approach to the understanding of folk traditions. Nor is Scheier
alone in his interest in twentieth-century folktale manifestations.
These two aspects among others receive treatment in the report of
the conference on American folk legend held in California in
1969,[43] and especially in the paper by Linda Degh entitled 'The
"Belief Legend" in Modern Society.' I do not intend here to
elaborate on this interest in modern folktales; but it is worth
pointing out that such interest, emphasizing as it does that man's
tendency to create folktales is as much a feature of modern as of
'primitive' life, has implications for the study of the Old Testament. As understood by the Victorians, and by Gunkel and
Frazer, folklore tended to create a gulf between the Old Testament
and the modern reader. If the Old Testament was full of traces of
folklore, this was evidence of the primitive belief and primitive
understanding of the world that characterized the Old Testament
period, in contrast to present-day enlightened civilization. However, if folktales are not just the preserve of the primitive, but are
a living force in a scientific age within societies that either practise
the 'higher' religions or claim to have grown out of the need for
religion altogether; and further, if they express needs that modern
man has in common with 'primitive' man, then we might be able

[42] K. Scheier, 'Zur Funktion von Volkserzahlungen,' in *Internationaler
Kongress* (ed. Ranke), pp. 370–7.
[43] W. D. Hand (ed.), *American Folk Legend*.

to understand the place of folktale in the Old Testament in a more positive way than hitherto.

Before drawing out this last remark, however, another development of interest to Old Testament study should be noted. Reference has already been made to Richard M. Dorson's monumental book *The British Folklorists*.[44] Probably nobody has done more than Dorson in recent years to put folklore studies in America on a proper scientific footing,[45] and he is a writer who deserves the closest attention from Old Testament scholars. In an article published in 1968, in the 60th birthday *Festschrift* for Kurt Ranke, Dorson addressed himself to the problem of the historical accuracy of oral tradition.[46] He reviewed the controversies that had raged on this topic among folklorists, among students of Icelandic sagas, and among anthropological students of Polynesian tradition. One of his most interesting demonstrations was the way in which the discussion had been compartmentalized. 'Each discipline has examined the issue in its own terms in seeming oblivion of the similar discussion being carried on elsewhere.'[47] Even the book on oral tradition by the anthropologist Vansina[48] had largely ignored the folklore contribution to the subject, and Dorson urged that the folklorist had an important role in such discussions because of his training in the recognition of typical motifs of traditions, and because of his first-hand experience of investigating and collecting oral traditions. Old Testament scholars can, perhaps, feel relieved that they are not the only ones who are unaware of what neighbouring disciplines are doing in related fields of importance; but it must also be clear that if folklore studies do have a key role to play in the understanding of oral traditions, and if folklore studies are gaining new insights with the help of other disciplines such as social psychology, then Old Testament scholarship must make a really determined effort to disprove in the future Gaster's complaint that 'the vast majority of biblical scholars have been slow

[44] See note 3.
[45] See his collection of articles in R. M. Dorson, *American Folklore and the Historian*, Chicago, 1971.
[46] R. M. Dorson, 'The debate over the Trustworthiness of Oral Tradition History,' in F. Harkort, K. C. Peeters, and R. Wildhaber (eds.), *Volksüberlieferung, Festschrift für Kurt Ranke zur Vollendung des 60. Lebensjahres*, Göttingen, 1968, pp. 19–36. Reprinted in R. M. Dorson, *Folklore: Selected Essays*, Bloomington, 1972, pp. 199–224.
[47] Idem., p. 32. [48] Jan Vansina, *Oral Tradition*, London, 1965.

to appreciate the implications of a folkloristic approach' to the Old Testament.

Apart from the implications of folklore studies for assessing the historic value of oral traditions, the other area of importance with regard to the Old Testament seems to me to be the understanding of crude supernatural elements in narratives.[49] In the Old Testament, bushes burn and are not consumed, pillars of cloud and fire journey from one place to another, serpents and asses speak, and so on. How are such events to be understood? Of course, it may be that these things actually happened; but if one takes the view that they did not happen, but are rather symbolic elements in narratives, the possibility of the miraculous at any level is not thereby being denied. The issue is not whether there are such things as miracles, but whether elements in the Old Testament narratives such as those just mentioned record actual miraculous happenings, or are a way of expressing in symbolic language what is believed to be true about God—e.g. that he guides and protects his people (the pillars of cloud and fire), and calls people to perform special tasks (Moses and the burning bush). Perhaps the point will be clearer if we recall Koch's point that saga and legend stand closer to metaphysics than does history. If we suppose that the Hebrews, without formulating in philosophical terms what we would call the immanence and transcendence of God, nevertheless experienced God as immanent and transcendent, the question is posed as to how this experience was expressed by them. The suggestion here is that as the oral traditions of God's saving acts were circulated among the Hebrews, they were shaped according to typical motifs and forms of folk traditions. But because such forms and motifs express the deepest hopes and needs of a people, their influence on the narratives about God's saving acts enabled these traditions to recount for the ancient Israelites not only pure information about these happenings, but also enabled a theological interpretation to be held in and with them.

If this is correct, then the task of Old Testament interpretation is not to try to rationalize incidents such as the burning bush and the pillars of cloud and fire, attempting to describe the burning bush as a sunset behind the bush, and the pillars of fire and cloud as volcanic activity. Rather the origin of such elements is to be

[49] See now my attempt to work out the following paragraphs in my book *The Supernatural in the Old Testament*, Guildford, 1976.

sought in folk motifs, and their function must be seen as theological symbols.

What is called for, then, is a balanced new look at the possible influence of folklore in the Old Testament. Such a new look will not want either to prove that everything in the Old Testament is history or that nothing is history; but when a sober estimate has been reached of the historicity of a narrative, then will be examined the possible ways in which folklore and oral transmission have helped the narrative to express the historical in terms of ancient Israel's belief in the divine.

5

Tribes, Clans and Groups

The 1967 Spring Meeting of the American Ethnological Society took as its subject 'The Problem of Tribe' and the proceedings were published in 1968 under the title *Essays on the Problem of Tribe*.[1] The contributors did their utmost to emphasize the ambiguity of the word 'tribe' as used in anthropology. One contributor exclaimed 'If I had to select one word in the vocabulary of anthropology as the single most egregious case of meaninglessness, I would have to pass over "tribe" in favour of "race." I am sure, however, that "tribe" figures prominently on the list of putative technical terms ranked in order of degree of ambiguity as reflected in multifarious definitions.'[2] Another contributor noted that 'tribe was variously used to refer to any primitive group, a primitive group with sodalities, especially sibs; a primitive group with or without sibs, but below the level of chiefdom; any political unit below the level of statehood; people speaking interintelligible dialects; groups with the "same" culture; groups with a common name; and groups with various combinations of traits in common, especially language, culture and name.'[3]

The reason for this ambiguity is not difficult to find. It has 'grown out of the intuitive, or predefinitional use of terms as observers, both trained and untrained, have reported their data with social terms that were already in common use but had not been defined precisely.'[4] This statement can, perhaps, be made

---

[1] June Helm (ed.), *Essays on the Problem of Tribe*, Washington, 1968.

[2] M. H. Fried, 'On the Concepts of "Tribe" and "Tribal Society," ' in *Essays on the Problem of Tribe*, pp. 4–5.

[3] Gertrude E. Dole, 'Tribe as the Autonomous Unit,' in *Essays on the Problem of Tribe*, p. 83.   [4] Dole, op. cit., p. 83.

clearer by an example. According to the *Oxford English Dictionary*, the word 'tribe' came into the English language as the result of Bible translation. The Greek versions of the Old Testament used the word *phyle* to designate the Hebrew 'tribe'; *phyle* had already been equated with the Latin *tribus*, and so this latter word was used in the Latin translations. From these translations, the word 'tribe' was first used in English, and used to denote the 'tribes' of Israel. It hardly needs to be said that at this time (the first *O.E.D.* reference is dated *c.* 1250) the nature of ancient Israelite organization was only vaguely, if at all, understood. Therefore, the word 'tribe' from the outset in English, designated groups of people whose social organization was not known. Once the word 'tribe' was in the language, it was applied to other, and often quite differing, social groups in many parts of the world. When such groups were more closely examined sociologically, because they had been labelled 'tribes,' attempts were made to define what tribes 'really were' on the basis of the findings of such investigations. Confusion resulted, for the single reason that it is doubtful whether these differing types of groups should have been labelled as 'tribes' in the first place. The whole exercise was an example of forcing a label on to complex phenomena that may have had *something* in common (e.g. that in some sense they were social groupings), but which had so many differences, that much more was lost by the way in which the label obscured these differences than was gained by the convenience of lumping the phenomena together under one common term.

Of course, the 'biblical sense' of 'tribe' was not the only meaning to have influence in English thought. The writers of the Classical world speculated about the nature of tribes and social organization, and such views had influence where Classics was studied.[5] But here, also, we must remember that Classical views were not without difficulty. The comment of one of the contributors to the American symposium on tribe is worth noting. 'A *tribus* was one of three segments of the Roman patriciate. Each segment was thought to have been a completely autonomous political unit in the past. As far as we know, neither of these conditions applied in ancient Rome: the word "tribe" lacked sociological rigour from

[5] C. H. J. de Geus, *De Stammen van Israel* (Diss.), Groningen, 1972, I, p. 122. See the English version, *The Tribes of Israel*, Assen/Amsterdam, 1976, p. 159.

its inception.'[6] It would be easy to multiply examples, from writings of the past hundred years, of the lack of rigour in the understanding of the word tribe. Perhaps the most salutary thing that one can do is to point out the havoc known to have been caused by some British colonial administrators who, convinced that 'tribes' must have chiefs, either created chiefs where none were needed, or concentrated their attentions on apparent chiefs whose functions were purely ceremonial and not at all political.

Returning to the American symposium on tribe, one point above all is clear: that it is extremely difficult to find criteria for defining groups of people for the purpose of sociological analysis and comparison. If residence in a particular area is the sole criterion, this may not do justice to the fact that those within the area who have come from outside the area and have married in, will have loyalties to their blood relatives. If blood ties are the sole criterion, this may not do justice to the question of residence. If the speaking of a common language is the criterion, problems are raised about how far a dialect is a different language, and so on. Gertrude Dole sums up these difficulties well when she advocates the use of a large number of terms to describe particular features of groups.

> Those who speak interintelligible languages are a *linguistic unit*; those who exploit a common territory, a *local group*; groups with similar cultures, a *culture unit*, or a *culture area* if they also occupy a single geographic area; groups who co-operate in ceremonial activities might be referred to as a *conference*; those who are bound by economic interaction might perhaps be called a *coecon*; and those who constitute an intermarrying population, a *connubium*.[7]

Dole thinks that the word 'tribe' must be retained in anthropology, and proposes to use it to describe 'autonomous units.' An 'autonomous unit' is one which has the right or power of self-government.[8]

[6] Fried, op. cit., p. 8.   [7] Dole, op. cit., p. 96.
[8] Dole, op. cit., p. 92 and p. 96, n. 4. De Geus, see II, p. 79, n. 142, appears to have misunderstood Dole completely here. What he gives as a quotation from Dole, p. 96, is in fact a mis-quotation. Thus: 'Tribe as an autonomous unit = an autonomous unit that is (a) a linguistic unit; (b) a local group; (c) a culture unit or culture area; (d) a conference

When we turn to consider the situation in Old Testament scholarship, it is perhaps not unfair to say that there is little awareness of the sort of problems discussed above. Students of Hebrew, or theologians who learn Hebrew, are invariably taught that the Hebrew words *šēḇeṭ* and *maṭṭeh* mean 'tribe.' They may also be taught that the word *mišpāḥāh* means 'family' or 'clan.' It is almost certain that students at this stage of their studies will have only the vaguest and unexamined ideas of what tribes are (if indeed they can be said to be anything). Some students may understand more by the word 'clan,' especially if they originate from certain parts of Ireland or Scotland, but most would be hard put to give a definition.[9] In Germany, the words *Stamm, Sippe, Unterstamm,* and even *Clan* are associated with the Hebrew words for social and kinship organization, although it is likely that most Germans are not clear what these words mean in relation to each other.[10]

However, Hebrew or no Hebrew, words like 'tribe' and *Stamm* are associated with the Old Testament, and although clearly the content of the Old Testament itself has been taken seriously in deciding the meanings of the terms in their relation to the Old Testament, the evidence contained in the latter is, as we shall see, ambiguous and fragmentary. Consequently, non-Old Testament senses of these words have often been imported into and imposed upon the discussion. It may be worth while to examine some examples.

As long ago as 1770, Michaelis suggested that Scottish clans,

---

(=co-operation in ceremonial activities); (e) a co-econ (=bound by economic interaction); (f) a connubium.' The mistake has been corrected in the English version, p. 158, n. 145.

[9] For discussions about 'clans' see R. Fox, *Kinship and Marriage*, Harmondsworth, 1967, especially pp. 49–50, 59, 134–6. Fox points out that although 'clan' etymologically (from the Gaelic *clann*) means the cognatic descendants of an eponymous ancestor, so that one can belong to clans on both one's father's and one's mother's side, there has been a tendency to use the word to describe only *unilineal* descent groups, as well as groups that are based on affiliation rather than descent, i.e. groups that are more like clubs than lineages.

[10] H. H. Meinhard, 'The Patrilineal Principle in Early Teutonic Kinship' in J. H. M. Beattie and R. G. Lienhardt (eds.), *Studies in Social Anthropology. Essays in Memory of E. E. Evans-Pritchard*, Oxford, 1975, notes (pp. 6 ff.) a certain amount of confusion in some scholarly German discussions involving the use of the word *Sippe*.

and ancient German tribes as described during the Roman Empire, could be guides to understanding the tribal organization of ancient Israel.[11] Over one hundred years later, Stade in his *Geschichte des Volkes Israel* repeated the same sort of comparison in order to explain the origin of the name Israel. The name Israel must have arisen, he maintained, in the way that all national names arise—by one tribe and its name gradually dominating all the other tribes in the area. Thus there must once have been a tribe called Israel.[12] This was a process that had taken place in ancient 'Germany.' German peoples such as the Franks and the Saxons came into being as the tribes of the Franks and the Saxons extended their power over neighbouring tribes in a particular area. Further, the resulting tribal unities came also to constitute religious unities. Just as the Saxons worshipped the God Saxnot, so the Israelites (the Israelites formed, in Stade's opinion, from the dominance of the tribe Israel over other tribes) adopted the worship practised by the original tribe Israel. Stade's analysis was accepted by R. Kittel,[13] although Kittel (not surprisingly) commented that it was odd that all reference to the tribe Israel had disappeared from the Old Testament if it really was the case that the people Israel had come into being as a result of the expansion of the tribe Israel.

If we pause to ask what the source of the information about the German tribes was, on which Michaelis, Stade and Kittel based their comparisons with ancient Israel, the answer is partly Tacitus's *Germania*, a book as well known in German education as Caesar's *Gallic Wars* was once known in British education.[14] From the scholarly angle, we must note that Tacitus was hardly a skilled and unbiased anthropological observer. On the contrary, it is likely that he wished to contrast Roman civilization with the German tribes to the advantage of the former. What we see, then, is an interesting chain of 'anthropological' evidence as applied to the Old Testament. It begins with the untrained observations of a Classical writer, and ends with the imposition of a theory on the

---

[11] J. D. Michaelis, *Mosaisches Recht*, para. 46.

[12] B. Stade, *Geschichte des Volkes Israel*, p. 124.

[13] R. Kittel, *Geschichte der Hebräer*, Gotha, 1888, pp. 17–18.

[14] Tacitus is explicitly mentioned by Michaelis in *Orientalische und Exegetische Bibliothek*, Vol. XI (1776), p. 8; and see also Meinhard, op. cit., p. 4.

Old Testament which makes nonsense of the evidence of the Old Testament itself.

Another way in which Old Testament scholarship has tried to understand the nature of ancient Hebrew society has been by way of comparison with Greek and Roman social organization. Stade's dependence on Fustel de Coulanges has been mentioned in an earlier chapter, and we must note here that Stade was also led by this dependence to equate the Hebrew tribe (*šēḇeṭ*) with the Roman *curia* and the Greek *phratra*, and the Hebrew 'family' (*mišpāḥāh*) with the Roman *gens* and the Greek *genos*.[15] On the other hand, a dictionary of biblical antiquities published in Germany at the end of the nineteenth century drew parallels between Hebrew 'tribes' and four Attic tribes (*phylai*) each of which was divided into three phratries, each phratry having thirty families. Thus as against Stade, the Hebrew *šēḇeṭ* was equated with the Greek *phyle* and the Hebrew *mišpāḥāh* with Greek *phratra*.[16] A number of other scholars also identified Hebrew *mišpāḥāh* with Greek *phratra* including B. Luther in an influential article published in 1901.[17] It is doubtful whether these writers had any real sociological knowledge about the nature of the Greek and Roman groups.

In recent scholarship, a Greek model has again been imposed upon the Old Testament, in order to explain ancient Israel's social and political organization at a particular point in its history, in Noth's theory of the amphictyony. Briefly, the theory states that during the period of the Judges, Israel was organized similarly to amphictyonic leagues known from Greece and Italy, as an amphictyony of tribes centred on a central sanctuary, and bound together by a common law and worship.[18] It is arguable that there is little or nothing in the Old Testament to suggest that Israel was thus organized at this period, and that the theory has originated through the imposition of Greek models on the Old Testament, and especially a model based on what is known about the Delphic League.

[15] Stade, op. cit., p. 402.

[16] E. C. H. Riehm, *Handwörterbuch des Biblischen Altertums*, Bielefeld and Leipzig, 1894², pp. 15–62 a–b.

[17] B. Luther, 'Die Israelitischen Stämme,' in *ZAW* (1901), p. 10.

[18] See M. Noth, *Das System der Zwolf Stämme Israels*, *BWANT*, IV:I (1930); idem *Geschichte Israels*, Göttingen, 1969⁷, pp. 83 ff., E.T. *History of Israel*, London, 1960², pp. 85–108.

GA

The theory of the amphictyony in Israel has come under attack,[19] and it would not be misleading to say that the main criticism has been that the Old Testament itself lacks evidence that there was an Israelite amphictyony. I would accept this criticism; but I would also want to make a different sort of criticism. The whole of the amphictyony theory takes it for granted that we know what the Israelite tribes were, and that we can make a cross-cultural comparison between these 'tribes' and the cities of the Greek amphictyonic leagues. But, in my view, we do not know sufficient about the groups concerned to make such comparisons. It is at this point that the dangers of the use of labels like 'tribe' and *'Stamm'* become most apparent. The cross-cultural comparison has been made and has been accepted by many Old Testament scholars as valid, mainly because the whole exercise has operated with largely unexamined concepts of 'tribe' and social grouping. It also needs to be asked whether scholars have looked closely enough at the *functions* of the Greek and alleged Israelite amphictyonies. According to some experts[20] the function of the Delphic League was to prevent any one member from having overriding power and authority over the sacred sanctuary and its oracle. Such power was thus divided equally among the members of the League. The same is not true of the alleged Israelite amphictyony, which far from protecting a central sanctuary against exploitation by one 'tribe,' knew frequent removals from one 'central sanctuary' to another.

Finally, an attempt will be made to illustrate another effect of the failure of Old Testament scholars to realize the need for concepts such as tribe to be analysed carefully, and in the light of anthropology. The issue will be the way in which tribal genealogies or stories concerning personified 'tribes' have been manipulated to reconstruct the history of the 'tribes.' A typical example

[19] G. Fohrer, 'Altes Testament—"Amphictyonie" und "Bund"?,' *Th.LZ*, 91 (1966), cols. 801–16, 893–904; G. W. Anderson, 'Israel: Amphictyony'; *'am; kāhāl; 'ēdāh*, in H. T. Frank and W. L. Reed (eds.), *Translating and Understanding the Old Testament*, 1970, pp. 135–51; R. de Vaux, 'La thèse de l'Amphictyonie Israelite' in *HTR*, 64 (1971), pp. 415–36. But see also R. Smend, 'Zur Frage der altisraelitischen Amphiktyonie' in *Evangelische Theologie*, 31, 1971, pp. 623–30.

[20] I am grateful to Dr. P. J. Rhodes of the Department of Classics, Durham University, for this information.

can once again be taken from Stade's *History of Israel*.[21] In reconstructing the early history of Israel, Stade proposed the principle that if a narrative relates the marriage of two eponymous ancestors, this denotes the uniting of two tribes or peoples. Further, if a tribe unites with a tribe more important than itself, the former tribe is described in the narrative as 'wife' and the latter tribe as 'husband.' Thus Leah, Rachel, Bilhah and Zilpah were all tribes that united with the tribe Jacob. Jacob, as the most dominant tribe, was called the husband, and the other tribes were called wives. Leah and Rachel, being more important than Bilhah and Zilpah, were called full wives, while the latter two tribes gained the description of handmaids.

Using the same materials, but different principles of interpretation, Steuernagel[22] argued that Israel originally consisted of four tribes, Leah, Rachel, Bilhah, and Zilpah. After the occupation of Canaan, these tribes broke down into smaller units. Rachel broke down into Joseph and Benjamin who became known as the *bnē* (sons of) Rachel; Leah broke down into Judah, Issachar, and Zebulun, who became known as *bnē* Leah. So far does Steuernagel's reconstruction differ from Stade's that whereas the latter held Jacob to be the all-dominating tribe in early Israel's history, Steuernagel found no place at all for Jacob in the early period, and attributed Jacob's prominent position in the tradition to later literary processes. It would be possible to cite many more varying reconstructions, but that is not my purpose here. My purpose is simply to show the extent to which the reconstruction of early Hebrew tribal history has been based on unexamined concepts. It is also worth asking whether the Old Testament in fact provides sufficient *historical evidence* to enable the movements of the elements of pre-settlement Israel to be reconstructed.

The Hebrew terms employed in the Old Testament to describe social groupings display a certain lack of consistency among themselves. Even the famous passage in Joshua 7:14–18 is not without its difficulties, which is noteworthy, because one might have hoped to get from such a passage a clear idea of Israelite social groupings. The passage concerns the detection of Achan by means of the lot, after Achan sinned by keeping some of the spoil from Jericho. In

[21] Stade, op. cit., pp. 114 ff.
[22] C. Steuernagel, *Die Einwanderung der israelitischen Stämme in Kanaan*, Berlin, 1901.

verse 14, Joshua is commanded to bring the people near, first, tribe by tribe (*šēḇeṭ*), then family by family (*mišpāḥāh*) of the tribe that is taken by the lot, then house by house (*bait*) of the family 'taken' and finally, man by man from the house 'taken.' However, in the sequel in vv. 16–18, we read (*R.V.*)

> So Joshua rose up early in the morning, and brought Israel near by their tribes; and the tribe of Judah was taken; and he brought near the family of Judah; and he took the family of the Zerahites; and he brought near the family of the Zerahites man by man; and Zabdi was taken; And he brought near his household man by man; and Achan, the son of Carmi, the son of Zabdi, the son of Zerah, of the tribe of Judah was taken.

It will be seen that Judah is here called both a tribe and a family, and that in this verse the word family therefore denotes both a larger and a smaller group. Also, there is a discrepancy between v. 14 and v. 17 as to whether the family is to be brought near by households, or man by man. It is understandable that with the support of ancient authorities, more recent translations (e.g. *N.E.B.*) have made vv. 16–17 conform with v. 14.[23] Thus the *families* (plural, not singular as in *R.V.*) of Judah are brought near and the family of the Zerahites is brought near by households. This may well be right; but the traditional Hebrew text contains the more difficult reading, and it is easier to suppose that the ancient authorities who differ from the traditional Hebrew text have made vv. 16–17 conform to v. 14 as to suppose that vv. 16–17 have been corrupted in such an obviously incongruous way. That the terms *šēḇeṭ*, *mišpāḥāh* and *bēt 'āḇ* do not possess the precision implied from Joshua 7:14 is clear from other examples. At Exodus 6:14 ff. the terms *mišpāḥāh* and *bēt 'āḇ* seem to be interchangeable. At Judges 17:7 Judah is described not as *šēḇeṭ* but as a *mišpāḥāh* while at Judges 20:12 a *šēḇeṭ* appears to be a subdivision of a tribe of Benjamin. At Amos 3:1 the whole people of Israel is called a *mišpāḥāh*. At Judges 6:15, the term *'eleḵ* normally meaning 'a thousand' in the context of military organization is used

---

[23] A similar procedure is adopted by scholars who wish to use this passage as the basis for assertions about Hebrew society. So most recently, H. W. Wolff, *Anthropologie des Alten Testaments*, pp. 309 ff., E.T. *Anthropology of the Old Testament*, pp. 214 ff.

to denote some sort of social grouping. (It is rendered 'family' by the *R.V.* and 'clan' by the *N.E.B.*)

One possible way of explaining this imprecision in terms is by maintaining that by the time the Hebrew Bible reached its final literary form, the precision of the terms had been forgotten.[24] But such imprecision is not peculiar to the Hebrew language. In his review of Robertson Smith's *Kinship and Marriage*, Nöldeke complained about the imprecision of Arab terminology. The same Arabic terms *qabîla*, *batn* and *fāḥiḏ* could denote not only large tribes, but also divisions within tribes. Even where Arab writers themselves tried to define these terms, the definitions only partly corresponded to reality.[25] Similar difficulties are known to modern anthropologists,[26] and should not surprise us if we remember what was urged in the first part of this chapter, namely, that social groups are highly complex phenomena which can hardly be adequately explained by modern consciously sophisticated terms, let alone by the rough and ready terms to be found in 'natural' language.

Supposing that it were possible to define terms like *šēḇeṭ* and *mišpāḥāh* precisely, what would be gained ? This is an important question, because it is often assumed that all that has to be done to understand ancient Israelite organization is to try to define the Hebrew terms in question. In fact, this is a serious methodological mistake. A people is no more likely to have a vocabulary of kinship and social terms that expresses the *structure* of its society in the way in which a modern anthropologist would understand structure, than it is likely to have a vocabulary of linguistic terms that express what a structural linguist would understand by the *structure* of its language. As people are largely unaware of the structure of the languages they speak, so are they largely unaware of their social structures. Further, the actual sense of a social term may often depend on the non-linguistic context in which the speaker finds himself.

In his book on the Nuer, Evans-Pritchard has illustrated this last point admirably in connection with the Nuer word *cieng*. The passage is long, but deserves quotation.

[24] Thus J. Licht in *Encyclopedia Biblica*, Vol. 5, Jerusalem, 1968, cols. 582 ff.

[25] T. Nöldeke in *ZDMG*, 40 (1886), pp. 175–6, p. 158.

[26] Cp. E. E. Evans-Pritchard, *The Nuer*, Oxford, 1940, pp. 115–16, 135–8.

What does a Nuer mean when he says 'I am a man of such-and-
such a *cieng*' ? 'Cieng' means 'home,' but its precise significance
varies with the situation in which it is spoken. If one meets an
Englishman in Germany and asks him where his home is, he
may reply that it is in England. If one meets the same man in
London and asks him the same question he will tell one that his
home is in Oxfordshire, whereas if one meets him in that county
he will tell one the name of the town or village in which he
lives. . . . So it is with the Nuer. A Nuer met outside Nuerland
says that his home is *cieng Nath*, Nuerland. He may also refer
to his tribal country as his *cieng*, though the more usual expression for this is *rol*. If one asks him in his tribe what is his
cieng, he will name his village or tribal section according to the
context. . . . If asked in his village he will mention the name of
his hamlet or indicate his homestead or the end of the village in
which his homestead is situated. . . . *Cieng* thus means homestead, hamlet, village, and tribal sections of various dimensions.[27]

Of course, the word *cieng* is probably not an exact parallel to a
word like the Hebrew word *šēḇeṭ*. But Evans-Pritchard goes on to
say that the relativity of meaning of a word like *cieng* is also true
of all social and political groupings.

A man is a member of a political group of any kind in virtue of
his non-membership of other groups of the same kind. He sees
them as groups and their members see him as a member of a
group, and his relations with them are controlled by the
structural distance between the groups concerned. But a man
does not see himself as a member of that same group in so far
as he is a member of a segment of it which stands outside of
and is opposed to other segments of it. . . . Political values are
always, structurally speaking, in conflict. One value attaches a
man to his group and another to a segment of it in opposition to
other segments of it, and the value which controls his action is a
function of the social situation in which he finds himself . . .
whether and on which side a man fights in a dispute depends
on the structural relationship of the persons engaged in it, and
of his own relationships to each party.[28]

I shall return to this point shortly.

[27] *The Nuer*, p. 136.   [28] Op. cit., p. 137.

The present chapter has been so far largely negative. It has outlined the complexity of social groups, and the problems that anthropologists experience in trying to analyse and compare them. In contrast, it has shown how Old Testament study has tended to work on such matters from a dangerously over-simplified standpoint. Can anything positive be said? I would suggest three possible ways forward.

In the first place, the Old Testament contains a good deal of genealogical material, and information about kinship relations between people. An anthropological/structural analysis of this might yield better results than attempts to define terms like *šēbeṭ* and *mišpāḥāh*. But I am convinced that the work cannot be done by an Old Testament expert alone or an anthropologist alone—there must be co-operation, for the problems on both sides are immense.

Second, several recent publications have tried to illuminate the social background and organization of the ancient Near East, and these are to be welcomed as possibly throwing light on the Old Testament. One thinks of the works by Kupper, Buccellati, and Giveon, and smaller studies by Noth and Malamat.[29] But again one must sound a note of warning. If social groups are as complex and difficult to describe as I have argued, then this is as true of ancient Mari or of the Egyptian *shosu* as of other groups. Therefore some knowledge of anthropological theory is necessary for the right interpretation of these texts, and it would be a mistake simply to try to analyse the technical terms for social organization to be found in them, and then to read such results into the Old Testament. To put things another way, there is no point in substituting for the Greek and Roman models that were used at the end of the nineteenth century for the explication of Hebrew social terms, models taken from the ancient Near East, if the latter models are no more scientifically arrived at than the former. For the Mari and Egyptian texts are not the work of trained

[29] J.-R. Kupper, *Les nomades en Mésopotamie au temps des rois de Mari*, Liège-Paris, 1957; G. Buccellati, *Cities and Nations of Ancient Syria* (Studi Semitici 26), Rome, 1967. R. Giveon, *Les bédouins shosou des documents égyptiens*, Leiden, 1971; M. Noth, 'Die Ursprünge des alten Israel im Lichte neuer Quellen' in *Aufsätze zur biblischen Landes- und Altertumskunde*, Vol. 2, Neukirchen-Vluyn, 1971, pp. 245–72. A. Malamat, 'Aspects of Tribal Societies in Mari and Israel' in *Les Congrès et colloques de l'université de Liège*, Vol. 42, Liège, 1967, pp. 129–38.

anthropological observers, their social vocabulary will be ambiguous, and their sociological interpretation will be problematical.
* Third, some help might come from a *cautious* use of what is known about political organization in general by anthropologists. An example could be the explanation of Nuer political organization as quoted above from the writings of Evans-Pritchard. His stress on the complexity of social groupings, and the fact that a man's values and actions will depend on his relationship to other people and groups in a given situation, seems to me to provide a way of understanding Israel's political 'organization' at the time of the Judges. In the book of Judges, we have evidence of united action on the part of some of the 'tribes' (e.g. Judg. Ch. 5) but also evidence of opposition between 'tribes' (e.g. Judg. Ch. 12). This last fact is not easily explained by the amphictyony theory, but is quite plausible if one thinks of groups who can come together for united action and just as quickly find themselves at odds, depending on the circumstances. It would, perhaps, be unwise to press the Nuer model on to the book of Judges; but it is precisely the sophistication of the model which helps it to make sense of the Judges material.

As a conclusion to this chapter, two discussions about Hebrew tribes which *do* take account of recent anthropology will be considered. They are the discussions by Mendenhall[30] and de Geus.[31] The fact that in some quarters, Old Testament scholars are beginning to recognize the importance of anthropology, if only in matters of social organization, is very much to be welcomed. On some points, the two writers take up similar positions. Thus both condemn the idea that in biblical times the Hebrews were semi-nomads[32] and they thus reject comparisons with later semi-nomads. De Geus argues strongly that when the forebears of the Hebrews emerged into the historical period, they were sedentary agriculturalists, practising the herding of animals as an extension of their agricultural concerns. Again, both authors deny that the Hebrew tribes were held together by common blood, and both emphasize the territorial (Mendenhall adds the administrative)

[30] G. E. Mendenhall, *The Tenth Generation*, Baltimore, 1973, Ch. VII, 'Tribe and State in the Ancient World: The Nature of the Biblical Community.'
[31] C. H. J. de Geus, *De Stammen van Israel, passim.*
[32] de Geus, p. 97, English, p. 127; Mendenhall, pp. 4–5.

role of the Hebrew tribes.[33] Further, both recognize that tribes
are not a stage on the way to the evolution of the state. Tribes may
result from breakdowns of larger social units, or arise in a 'colonial'
situation if an area is conquered.[34] In other ways, their reconstructions diverge.

Mendenhall appears to be mainly dependent on one American
anthropologist,[35] whom, however, he does not follow slavishly.
Mendenhall emphasizes the dynamic nature of social organization, its change and continuity, and remarks (a) 'that a purely
formal analysis of ancient culture can yield neither good historical
description nor any adequate understanding of the dynamics of
historical change and continuity,'[36] and (b) 'that a tribe in early
historical societies has only incidental similarity to what is classified
as a tribe by modern anthropology, and is actually a typologically
early form of political structure the real nature and function of
which we know very little, even in the early Israelite federation.'[37]

Mendenhall's caution here is most refreshing, as is the way in
which he implicitly drops the word 'tribe,' and argues that we
must try to describe early Israel's political structure on the basis
of historical resources. However, when he tries to be more
positive, Mendenhall cannot avoid the use of a Classical model, or
of cross-cultural comparison. Just as the Roman *tribus* was a
political unit, he argues, so a Hebrew *šēḇeṭ* (= staff or club, a sign
of authority) is that over which the staff of office rules, and is thus
an administrative unit.[38] He also takes a Roman model in terms of
which to understand the situation of Palestine in the fourteenth
to twelfth centuries B.C., when he argues that the seizure of the
fortified towns by external superior power groups upset the balance
between the villages and the fortified towns, thus forcing the
villages to form social units of sufficient size to counterbalance the
towns. Out of such a disturbance the Israelite federation emerged,

---

[33] de Geus, pp. 113–16, English, 178–9, 184–5; Mendenhall, pp. 144 f.
[34] de Geus, pp. 101–2; English, 188 ff.; Mendenhall, pp. 131–2.
[35] On E. R. Service's *Primitive Social Organisation: An Evolutionary
Perspective*, New York, 1972. For a critique of aspects of Service's
position, see H. S. Lewis, 'Typology and Process in Political Evolution,'
in *Essays on the Problem of Tribe.*
[36] Mendenhall, p. 177.   [37] Op. cit., p. 185.
[38] Op. cit., p. 184–5. A definition of tribe on the basis of the etymology
of *šēḇeṭ* has a long pedigree. It is found, for example, in E. C. H. Riehm
Handwörterbuch des Biblischen Altertums, 1894, col. 1562 a.

though it was based not on force of arms, but on the moral and ethical force of the covenant.[39]

De Geus makes an attempt to understand the Hebrew terms *bēt 'āḇ*, *mišpāḥāh* and *šēḇeṭ*. A *bēt 'āḇ* was an exogamous (marrying out) extended family, and thus needed to be dependent (at least, for marriage purposes!) on a larger unit, the *mišpāḥāh*, translated as *sibbe* by de Geus. (For want of a better word, the English 'clan' will be used for the Dutch *sibbe*.) The clan was an endogamous (marrying in) unit, and was the fundamental unit of social organization in ancient Israel. From the point of view of land owners, the clan coincided with the town, so that it was both a territorial and a social kinship group. De Geus prefers to speak of tribe in the same breath as people. The tribes or people of Israel were a voluntary association of clans, comprising a *connubium* (an intermarrying group) and a *forum* (a group recognizing a common law). However, the association of clans into tribes or people depended on historical circumstances, and fluctuated to some extent. His view of the nature of Israelite tribes leads de Geus to a negative verdict on Noth's theory of the (tribal) amphictyony.

Judging from the bibliographical data supplied by de Geus and Mendenhall the former is more familiar with recent anthropological writings on tribes than the latter; but it is likely that Mendenhall has achieved more anthropologically. Although de Geus is aware that the term 'tribe' has problems of definition, he does not seem to take the same point for clan, and in spite of the imprecision of the Hebrew terms, he hopes to identify and describe a *bēt 'āḇ* and a *mišpāḥāh*. He also overlooks the non-linguistic factors which make it difficult to describe such terms.[40] Mendenhall, on the other hand, has allowed for a much more dynamic social situation in ancient Israel.

In my opinion, the views of both these scholars will have to be corrected and supplemented. For one thing, both attribute little historical value to the biblical genealogies, and while this may be correct, there is more to be done anthropologically on this front in relation to ancient Israel than either Mendenhall or de Geus

---

[39] Op. cit., pp. 185 ff. Mendenhall follows (not uncritically) the account of relations between *vici* (pastoral villages) and *oppidum* (fortified town) within a territory (*pagus*) as given in *Pauly's Real-Encyclopädie der classischen Altertumswissenschaft*.

[40] See above, n. 26.

attempt.[41] The problem is not merely to bring anthropological insights to bear on the social organization of Israel during the two centuries before the establishment of the monarchy, but rather to examine all the traditions about tribes and genealogies, etc., in the Old Testament, from Genesis to Chronicles in the light of anthropology. As stated earlier in this chapter, this will only be done adequately by some form of inter-disciplinary co-operation.

[41] A substantial attempt in this direction has now been made in R. R. Wilson, *Genealogy and History in the Biblical World*, New Haven, 1977.

6

Structural Anthropology

Structural anthropology is a development within social anthropology which began some thirty years ago. It is inseparably linked with the name of the French sociologist Claude Lévi-Strauss. Lévi-Strauss himself has written nothing, to my knowledge, about the Old Testament. Indeed, he has said that the Old Testament is too fragmentary, and that its traditions have been subjected too much to theological re-interpretation to be the subject of structural analysis.[1] But he has had an influence on anthropological theory that deserves attention in its own right, and which will make a useful conclusion to the present book. This chapter will first consider Lévi-Strauss's work, and second, see how it has been applied and how it might apply to the Old Testament.

At the outset, it must be said that structural anthropology is part of the larger phenomenon of structuralism, and that the latter is also to be found in disciplines such as mathematics, physics, biology, psychology and linguistics.[2] It should also be pointed out that structuralism differs to some extent as between and even in some cases within these disciplines,[3] and that therefore the terms 'structure,' 'structural' and 'structuralism' must be used with care. In the interests of simplicity, I shall not attempt to define structuralism,[4] but will hope to demonstrate in the course of the chapter what it is as applied to social anthropology.

[1] See Lévi-Strauss in *Esprit*, November, 1963, pp. 611 ff.
[2] See the survey by J. Piaget, *Structuralism*, London, 1971, translated from *Le Structuralisme*, Paris, 1968.
[3] Piaget, op. cit., pp. 97 ff., distinguishes between 'global' and 'analytic' structuralism in social anthropology.
[4] For a definition, see Piaget, op. cit., pp. 3 ff.

Lévi-Strauss has a number of aims, but for present purposes, I shall concentrate on what constitutes the most distinctive aspect of structuralism.[5] While he is completely opposed to the global approach to anthropology practised by the evolutionists in the nineteenth century, Lévi-Strauss is also ill at ease with the concentration on individual societies, and the reticence to make generalizations, that came about in the fieldwork and functionalist phase of social anthropology. He is therefore concerned to find a way of making generalizations about anthropological data, while avoiding the mistakes of scholars such as Frazer.

Perhaps the clearest expression of this is to be found in an article first published in 1944.[6] The article begins with a vigorous criticism of the evolutionists, and their concept of the primitive.

Few anthropologists would admit today that human groups displaying an extreme primitiveness either in the field of material culture or that of social organization can teach us something about early stages of the evolution of mankind. Primitiveness in one field often goes with a great sophistication in another, as shown by the Australian refinements concerning kinship. Since these primitive peoples have their own history, it would be a serious mistake to think that it may be discounted because we know nothing of it. The partial similarities which archaeological remains allow us to infer between primitive societies and those of pre-historic man, while they remain sheer hypotheses, do not preclude the tremendous differences which may have existed in fields outside of the archaeologist's reach.[7]

Having disposed of much of the theory that characterized what this book has called the second period of anthropology, Lévi-Strauss turns his attack against those anthropologists who have

[5] For a different approach to Lévi-Strauss, see my article 'Structural Anthropology and the Old Testament,' in *BSOAS*, Vol. XXXIII, 1970, pp. 590 ff., and the literature there cited.

[6] C. Lévi-Strauss, 'The Social and Psychological Aspects of Chieftainship in a Primitive Tribe: the Nambikuara of Northwestern Mato Grosso.' First publ. in *Transactions of the New York Academy of Sciences* 7 (1944), pp. 16–32; reprinted in R. Cohen and J. Middleton (eds.) *Comparative Political Systems*, New York, 1967, pp. 45–62, to which reference is here made.

[7] Op. cit., p. 45.

concentrated on individual societies, and who have been reluctant to generalize about them.

Are we condemned, like new Danaids, to fill endlessly the sieve-like basket of anthropological science; in vain, pouring monographs over monographs without being able to collect a substance with a richer and denser value ?[8]

The answer to this is 'no.' While simpler societies than our own are not necessarily to be thought of as archaic, they nevertheless throw light 'on some basic forms of activity which are to be found, *always and everywhere*, as *prerequisites* for the existence of human society.'[9] Lévi-Strauss then proceeds to illustrate his point by describing how chieftainship works in a small Brazilian tribe.

The political organization of the tribe is of the simplest: the chief's function is to guide, direct and sustain his people, whether they are roaming through their hunting grounds, or spending the rainy season in camp. To assist him in his tasks he has the privilege of plural marriage, while the other men are restricted to one wife. The whole of his authority is based on the consent of his people, and an *exchange* between him and them.

Each man receives a wife from another man, but the chief receives several wives. In exchange, he offers to guarantee against need and danger, not to the individuals whose sisters or daughters he marries; not to those who will be deprived of a spouse by his polygamous right; but to the group, taken as a whole.[10]

The principle of *exchange* is taken further in a work published a few years later, *The Elementary Structures of Kinship*.[11] Lévi-Strauss sets out from the problem of incest, i.e. the fact that almost universally at all times, marriage between primary kin has been prohibited, and offenders severely punished.[12] What is the reason for this almost universal prohibition ? According to Lévi-Strauss, it is not that societies have decided to legislate against it

[8] Op. cit., p. 46.   [9] Op. cit., p. 46, italics mine.   [10] Op. cit., p. 60.
[11] *Les structures élémentaires de la parenté*, Paris, 1949, 1967². E.T. *The Elementary Structures of Kinship*, London, 1969.
[12] A distinction must be made here between *sexual relations* with primary kin, and *marriage* between primary kin, for although both may be equally prohibited, they are not necessarily the same thing. See Robin Fox, *Kinship and Marriage*, pp. 54 ff. Lévi-Strauss's position is concerned with incest in the sense of marriage with primary kin.

(this only raises the question *why* they have thus legislated); it is not based on the observation (if this is a correct observation) that in-breeding produces physical and mental defects; it cannot be satisfactorily explained by Freudian principles. Lévi-Strauss's view is that incest is almost universally prohibited because it contradicts the need for men to *exchange* women; further, this need for exchange is itself an expression of the basic structure of the human mind.

In all types of society, families cannot live in isolation if the society is to survive. If an unmarried farmer desires sons to help with his work and eventually inherit the farm, he must marry, i.e. take a woman from another family. If, after his marriage, he has daughters as well as sons, he will expect to give his daughters to other young men as wives; similarly, he will expect other families to provide wives for his sons. Thus, there is a reciprocity of exchange of women between men, which is vital to the maintenance of society. If families were completely isolated from each other, and all marriages were within close family groups, it could not be guaranteed that the right number of boys and girls would be born to enable the family grouping to survive.

Now it could be justly argued that the sort of exchange just described is a natural fact of life, and nothing to do with structures of the human mind. But some kinship systems are of astonishing complexity, with most elaborate rules for determining who may marry whom. It is Lévi-Strauss's belief that such cases indicate that we have to reckon with a 'patterning' in kinship systems, and that this patterning is the result of the human mind imposing various patterns on a basic and natural need for men to exchange women. A similar example can be found in language. Language represents the basic need for men to communicate with each other; but there are several thousand language systems in the world, all of them the result of a patterning deriving from the human mind. Indeed, it is to certain aspects of modern linguistics that Lévi-Strauss looks, in his search for an adequate method of understanding social data.

Ever since the posthumous publication in 1916 of F. de Saussure's *Course in General Linguistics*,[13] linguists have sought to

[13] F. de Saussure, *Cours de linguistique générale*, Paris and Lausanne, 1916. See the important study by E. F. K. Koerner, *Ferdinand de Saussure*, Braunschweig, 1973.

investigate *langue*, the system of language which underlies *parole*, the speech acts of individuals. In the study of phonology (the study of the basic sounds in languages) it has been discovered that the sounds used in all known languages can be described in terms of a dozen pairs of sounds, which are distinguished by the presence or absence of distinctive features. For example, 'p' and 'b' are such a pair, distinguished by the presence of 'voice' in the case of 'b,' and its absence in the case of 'p.' Lévi-Strauss makes no secret of the fact that he would like to achieve in social anthropology what phonologists have achieved in linguistics.[14] He would like to regard social *facts* as similar to *parole*, and he would like to describe them in terms of an underlying *system*, similar to the linguistic investigation of *langue*. This is why in *The Elementary Structures of Kinship* he tries to interpret all systems of kinship in terms of a simple system of exchange. It is still necessary to clarify, however, how Lévi-Strauss relates the system underlying social facts to the basic structure of the human mind.

It is a matter of continuing debate among linguistic experts and scientists whether the 'laws' which they formulate to describe and explain phenomena have any 'reality' of their own. Are such laws merely helpful generalizations with a certain amount of predictive power, or do they correspond to some deeper reality? Lévi-Strauss believes that with regard to linguistics and social anthropology, the 'laws' by which phenomena can be explained are more than helpful generalizations; they mirror the basic structure of the human mind. In the description of language sounds, phonologists have used the binary principle, in which things are grouped in pairs according to the presence or absence of distinctive features (see the example with 'p' and 'b' above). The binary principle is also much used in computer science, where information is stored and retrieved.[15] For example, an appropriately programmed computer can identify a single word in a dictionary of 250,000 words by a code of only 18 numbers, the code consisting of the numbers 0 and 1, which are equivalent to 'no' and 'yes.' The programme is arranged so that the code is the answer to a series of questions: is the word in the first half of the dictionary? (1 for 'yes,' 0 for 'no');

[14] See *Structural Anthropology*, London, 1968, Chapters ii–v.
[15] The example following is taken from C. Cherry, *On Human Communication*, Cambridge, Massachusetts, 1966², p. 50.

Is it in the first half of that section? and so on. Now there is reason to suppose that the human brain itself works on a similar principle in storing and retrieving information, and in other activities,[16] and thus it is that Lévi-Strauss can assert that the binary system by which the phonologist describes the sounds of languages, and which Lévi-Strauss hopes to apply to social data, is more than a convenient method of description and generalization; in fact, it derives from the nature of the human mind.

Lévi-Strauss's position as so far outlined can be summed up as follows. The universal prohibitions of incest can only be satisfactorily understood in terms of the need for men to exchange women. This system of exchange, like language, is a system of communication. In linguistics, especially in phonology, it has been possible to describe aspects of very diverse languages in terms of simple 'laws' based on the binary principle. It ought to be possible to do the same for kinship systems and other social phenomena. Since the binary principle is a characteristic of the structure and functioning of the human mind, explanatory models based on the binary principle correspond to the structure of the mind. It is the working of the human mind in a binary way which produces the languages, the kinship networks and other social facts which the anthropologist studies.

We may break off from the main discussion to say that although all this may seem to have taken us a long way from the Old Testament, we can in fact find in the Old Testament three clear examples of 'binary activity.' In Jos. 7:16–18 and 1 Sam. 14:40–2 (see *R.S.V.* and *N.E.B.*), the 'lot' is used to discover a culprit, and in I Sam. 10:19–21 it is used to select a king. Although the precise nature of the 'lot' is not known, it is clear that it worked in exactly the same way as the computer programme mentioned above. The 'lot' had, in effect, the answers 'yes' and 'no,' and it was used in such a way as to break down the people involved, into groups of ever diminishing size, until the suspect or the chosen individual was indicated. These examples make it overwhelmingly probable that underlying at least the social activity that involved the 'lot' in ancient Israel, were the binary discriminations of the human mind. It is interesting to note that some writers have regarded Jos. 7:16–18 as evidence for a period when ancient

[16] Cherry, op. cit., pp. 276 ff.

HA

Israelites were unable to discriminate clearly between things that are distinct for 'moderns.'[17] However, it would seem that to manipulate a lot which could answer only 'yes' or 'no' so as to single out an individual from a large body of people required a considerable degree of analytical thinking on the part of somebody, and that the burden of proof should rest upon those who would argue that Israelites in this period did not think analytically, to substantiate their case.

Lévi-Strauss has worked out his interest in the binary nature of mental operations in essays such as 'The Science of the Concrete' in *The Savage Mind*. Here, he shows how 'primitives' have a remarkable knowledge of the world about them, and know, for example, the medical properties of herbs and plants. This knowledge is based upon observation and trial and error, and underlying it is the fact that the 'primitive' organizes the world about him in terms of binary distinctions: high/low, heavy/light, soft/hard and so on. Indeed, Lévi-Strauss asserts that basically, there is no difference between the way the 'primitive' divides the world into categories, and the way the modern scientist organizes things into categories on the basis of similarity and difference. Where 'primitive' and scientific activities differ, as of course they do, the differences lies not in the mental processes involved, but in the materials used (and one ought to add that the modern scientist does his work as part of a scientific community, and in accordance with its paradigms). Thus Lévi-Strauss can say:

> The difference lies not in the quality of the intellectual process, but in the nature of the things to which it is applied. This is well in agreement with the situation known to prevail in the field of technology: what makes a steel axe superior to a stone axe is not that the first one is better made than the second. They are equally well made, but steel is quite different from stone.[18]

[17] H. W. Robinson used the Achan incident of Jos. 7 as the main support for one of his senses of 'corporate personality.' See my article in *J.T.S.*, XXI, 1970, pp. 3–5, where it is maintained that Robinson thought that the Hebrews had no developed sense of individuality at this time. See also G. von Rad, *Wisdom in Israel*, E.T., London, 1972, pp. 58–9, where the events of I Sam. 13–14 are held to imply a different way of understanding reality, as compared with the situation brought about by a 'decisive change' in the reign of Solomon.

[18] *Structural Anthropology*, p. 230.

Like the comments made above in regard to Jos. 7:16 18 and the other passages, Lévi-Strauss's position here, that although the actual classifications of 'primitives' may differ from those of modern scientists, the underlying discriminatory process is the same in both cases, is at odds with some of the views of Hebrew mentality described in Chapter III.

The aspect of Lévi-Strauss's position which has been most widely applied to the Old Testament has yet to be described here, but it follows on from what has just been said about classification. Myths (which Lévi-Strauss understands very broadly to include stories, legends, folktales, etc.) are 'products' of societies, and products which are expressed in language. Lévi-Strauss applies to 'myths' his belief that social data are based on the structure and functions of the human mind. Primitive man, says Lévi-Strauss, as well as classifying the world around him in terms of binary distinctions, is aware of many anomalies that defy classification. Man knows himself to be part of nature, and to have much in common with animals; but man is also different, in that he has created a culture, and has been able to pass on cultural achievements from one generation to the next. Again, man is conscious of the paradox of life and death, in that in the world of nature, he knows that death is a necessary prelude to life; but in the case of man, the very awareness of what it is to be alive, and the fear of death, seem to place man in a different position from animals with regard to life and death.

Lévi-Strauss believes that in myths, the human mind explores and resolves these dilemmas, at levels below those of conscious thought. In many South American Indian myths, the distinction between nature and culture is 'blurred' by stories that relate how mankind stole the secret of fire (the supreme symbol of culture) from the jaguar, so that the animals for ever lost the secret.[19] In analysing myths, Lévi-Strauss pays less attention to their narrative sequence than to elements or characters in the story that can be contrasted as 'binary oppositions.' Such a method seems very strange at first sight, and its results are also strange (an illustration will be given below); but the method also draws attention to elements in the narrative that are usually overlooked or ignored by the usual methods of interpretation.

[19] See *Le cru et le cuit*, Paris, 1964; E.T. *The Raw and the Cooked*, London, 1970.

This is not the place in which to provide a detailed critique of Lévi-Strauss's structural anthropology, especially as there are many critiques written by properly qualified scholars.[20] By way of summary, it can be said that critics have questioned the validity of applying procedures from linguistics to the analysis of social data; they have pointed out that Lévi-Strauss's theories can be neither proved nor disproved, and that ultimately, they reduce everything to the functioning of the human mind. However, such criticisms, while fair in themselves, cannot alter the fact that Lévi-Strauss's writings can make a profound impression of artistry and creativity upon their readers, shedding new light in unexpected places, and putting into new perspective things that one thought one understood. Lévi-Strauss may be mistaken in some of his central assertions, but as a result of his work, social anthropology will never be quite the same again.

Lévi-Strauss has not applied his methods to the Old Testament.[21] It has been left to other social anthropologists to do this, and mainly, they have applied to the Old Testament his methods of interpreting 'myths.'[22] A recent example is provided by D. F. Pocock's 'North and South in the Book of Genesis.'[23] Although Pocock refers to Lévi-Strauss only in a footnote, and speaks about his exposition in terms of 'symbolic geography,' the essay is, in fact, a good example of a treatment of a biblical text that owes much to Lévi-Strauss. The author begins by stating his opinion that a striking feature of the narrative of the 'fall' in Genesis 3 is the introduction of a territorial element; life begins for the human race only after the expulsion from the garden. For the Hebrews, according to Pocock, this story of alienation from territory was especially significant, because they had to face a 'profound intellectual problem ... the problem posed by the lack of an immemorial base such as almost all other recorded peoples have enjoyed. ... In the Yahwistic creation myth the Hebrews repre-

[20] The most searching critique that I have seen, together with a full bibliography, is by Bob Scholte, 'The Structural Anthropology of Claude Lévi-Strauss' in *Handbook of Social and Cultural Anthropology*, pp. 637–716.

[21] See my *Myth in Old Testament Interpretation*, pp. 107–8.

[22] Examples are given, op. cit., pp. 109 ff.

[23] J. H. M. Beattie and R. G. Lienhardt, *Studies in Social Anthropology*, pp. 273–84.

sent themselves as literally *déracinés*, as a people created alien.[24] This assertion leads on to an investigation of the way in which *territory*, especially in geographical movements recorded in Genesis, express 'for the recensionists,' moral values, in which a movement from south to north has a redemptive character, offsetting the alienation implied in the 'fall' story.

Thus, Abraham comes from the north-east, and Isaac gets a son from there. In the south, however, Abraham twice and Isaac once have to resort to trickery in order to preserve their lives, and they do this by passing off their wives as their sisters. Although they have journeyed to the south in search of material prosperity, the south endangers their marital prosperity. The north–south opposition continues in the story of Jacob and Esau, where the latter marries women from the south and is disinherited, while Jacob journeys north for his two wives. But the trick played by Jacob on Esau is now played by Laban on Jacob. Whereas the younger brother outwitted the elder, Jacob is not allowed to marry Laban's younger daughter before he has married Leah, and the precedence of the elder over the younger is restored. Jacob soon finds himself on the run towards the south; he effects a reconciliation with Laban at Mizpah Galeed, after which he moves northwards[25] towards his great encounter in the wrestling at Jabbok (Gen. 32:23–32) where Jacob becomes the nation Israel. In the final chapters of Genesis, the Israelites move southwards into Egypt to escape famine. Once again, the south proves to be a snare, for it results in the oppression from which a move to the north in the Exodus is required, in order to bring redemption.

Pocock's exposition has all the strengths and weaknesses of a structural anthropological analysis of a text. It makes compelling reading, and suggests ways of looking at certain details that would never have occurred to one used to the standard methods of biblical interpretation. On the other hand, there is no way of proving that the exegesis is correct, or that the recensionists did indeed see redemptive significance in a movement from the south to the north. Indeed, the Old Testament scholar will want to ask how, in this case, we are to understand the movement to the north when Israelites from the northern kingdom were taken to captivity to Assyria in 732 and 721. Also, although strictly speaking Babylon is to the east of Judah, one reached it by travelling northwards in

[24] Op. cit., pp. 274–5.   [25] Op. cit., pp. 282–3.

the first instance, so that the exile to Babylon in the sixth century involved a movement northwards, and the return, a journey southwards. If the recensionists of the book of Genesis in its final form worked during or just after the time of the Babylonian exile, as is commonly believed, we may be excused for being puzzled that they should have seen the significance in the movement to the north that Pocock wishes to maintain.

It is unlikely that structuralist interpretation of Old Testament texts on the basis of *anthropological* theories will commend itself to Old Testament scholars, for the reason that they have already embraced *literary* structuralist theories.[26] Although both types of structuralism have their roots in structural linguistics as initiated by de Saussure, literary structuralism avoids Lévi-Strauss's view that 'myths' are attempts to resolve basic human problems, which ultimately rest on the nature of the human mind. On the contrary, in some of its forms, literary structuralism offers a method of interpretation which allows a full part to the 'discovery' of structures by the modern interpreter, regardless of the question whether they were originally intended by the writer or writers.[27]

The main contribution of anthropological structuralism to Old Testament studies will come, in my view, in the following ways. It will teach Old Testament scholars something about the classificatory system of reality implied in the Old Testament. This ought to make it impossible for Old Testament scholars to assert that the ancient Israelites experienced reality in an undifferentiated or 'confused' way. Secondly, Old Testament scholarship may learn something about the *symbolic* meaning of the Hebrew classification of reality, especially as this affects institutions such as sacrifice.

Significant work in this direction has been done by the social anthropologist Mary Douglas. In *Purity and Danger*,[28] she argues that the unclean creatures described in Lev. 11 and Deut. 14 are to be understood in terms of the classification system implied in Genesis 1. In the creation story, there is a basic three-fold classification, based on the earth, the waters, and the sky. In

---

[26] See my article 'Recent Literary Structuralist Approaches to Biblical Interpretation' in *The Churchman*, vol. 90 (1976), pp. 165–77.

[27] See 'Recent Literary Structuralist Approaches to Biblical Interpretation', p. 168.

[28] 'The Abominations of Leviticus,' in *Purity and Danger*, pp. 41–57.

Leviticus, the creatures proper to each category are defined as follows. Proper earth creatures are those with four legs which walk, jump, or hop. In the waters, the proper creatures swim with fins, and in the sky, the proper creatures are two-legged fowls which fly with wings. Some of the unclean animals do not fit these schemes. Four-legged creatures which fly (e.g. insects) are unclean, as are creatures with two hands and two legs but which go on all fours. Also unclean are creatures that creep, crawl, or swarm upon the earth, or 'swarm' in the waters. In the case of swine, Professor Douglas argues that they are unclean because they do not conform to a classificatory rule according to which certain animals must both chew the cud and have cloven hooves.

The unclean creatures in the Old Testament have been regarded as ancient Israelite insights into hygiene, or as a deliberate avoidance of animals connected with the religious practices of the Canaanites. Professor Douglas appeals to anomalies in classification as the origin for the prohibition of certain creatures. However, she is not merely interested in the origin of the prohibitions, but in the symbolic meaning of the code of prohibitions. She believes that the code was, for the Hebrew, a way of expressing loyalty to God, in dealings with the animal kingdom. 'The dietary laws would have been like signs which at every turn inspired meditation on the oneness, purity and completeness of God.'[29] What is left of Lévi-Strauss's structural anthropology here, is that Professor Douglas has accepted his view that reality is ordered in terms of oppositions and classifications by the Hebrews. She has gone beyond him in seeing in the practical application of a classificatory system, a social code embodying and expressing the Hebrew view of the dependence of the natural order upon the creative power of God. It may be argued that her understanding of the unclean creatures is no more capable of being shown to be correct than Pocock's exposition of Genesis. While this must be conceded, it seems to me that the two things are of a different order. It was argued above that the use of the 'lot' in ancient Israel implied a sophisticated analysis of groups in a binary manner, and the classificatory scheme seems to be clearly present in Genesis 1. Also, it should occasion no surprise that the Genesis scheme should not be able to avoid creating anomalies. All in all, Douglas's way of accounting for the origin of the unclean creatures is at

[29] Op. cit., p. 57.

least as convincing as theories put forward by Old Testament
scholars, and is probably better able than these latter to account
for most, though not all, of the prohibitions. Whatever Old
Testament scholars may think of Douglas's treatment, in its
symbolic aspect, it is in line with the current anthropological
interest in symbols and their interpretation.[30]

As a final example of interpretation of the Old Testament inspired by structural anthropology, reference can be made to an
article on aspects of sacrifice, by Douglas Davies.[31] Davies
devotes his attention to the use of 'space' in various rituals.
He distinguishes (as, of course, does the Old Testament) between
the camp (the sphere of ordered social relationships), outside the
camp (the sphere of the chaotic and the abnormal), and the holy
place. In the ritual of expelling and rehabilitating the 'leper' (Lev.
13–14) much use is made of these different spheres. The leper is
expelled from the camp, argues Davies, not only because his
affliction may be contagious, but primarily because his appearance
is disruptive and disturbing to those within the sphere of ordered
relationships. The ritual for his rehabilitation involves a gradual
process in which he is brought back into the camp, and allowed to
take his place once more in ordered social activity. Thus whatever
may be the individual psychological way in which the ritual was
regarded by those involved, the ritual also has a *symbolic social*
significance.

To conclude, Lévi-Strauss's theories with regard to kinship
and myth will probably have little influence in future Old Testament studies; but his work on classification, and its application to
social activities regarded as 'codes' embodying a people's understanding of reality, may prove to be of some importance for
understanding the Old Testament.

[30] For examples of this concern see Mary Douglas, *Natural Symbols*,
London, 1970, idem. (ed.) *Rules and Meanings*, Harmondsworth, 1973;
R. Firth, *Symbols Public and Private*, London, 1973; R. Willis (ed.),
The Interpretation of Symbolism, London, 1975.
[31] Douglas Davies, 'An Interpretation of Sacrifice in Leviticus' in
ZAW 89 (1977), pp. 387–99.

Postscript

Since the main text of this book was written, several relevant books and articles have appeared or come to the notice of the author; the purpose of this Postscript is to outline the most important of these.

In the concluding chapter,[1] it was suggested that because Old Testament scholars have become interested in *literary* structuralism, it was unlikely that they would make very much use of *anthropological* structuralism. However, in one regard, literary structuralism has led Old Testament experts to one of the areas discussed in this book, namely, folklore studies. The translation into English of V. Propp's *The Morphology of the Folktale*[2] has made scholars aware of the structural (or formal) school in folklore studies. Propp's thesis, based upon extensive analysis of Russian folktales, is that such tales can be described in terms of a limited number of roles (e.g. the hero, the villain) and functions (e.g. the hero goes into exile, the hero returns, the hero makes use of magical agencies). Analyses based upon this approach have begun to be applied to the Old Testament, and it has been noted, for example, that Propp's functions can be applied to the Jacob narrative.[3]

If such applications prove to be convincing, it may become necessary to reconsider some of the standard approaches in Old Testament study to narratives such as the Jacob cycle, approaches that see the finished product as amalgams of originally separate

---

[1] See above, p. 112.

[2] V. Propp, *Morphology of the Folktale*, Austin, Texas, 1968[2]. See also E. K. and P. Maranda, *Structural Models in Folklore*, The Hague, 1971.

[3] See A. de Pury, *Promesse divine et légende culturelle dans le cycle de Jacob*, Paris, 1975.

tribal or territorial traditions. If Jacob leaving his home to live
with Laban can be shown to be an example of a typical structural
element of folktales in which we have no reason to suspect the
combination of separate territorial traditions, it will need to be
questioned whether, in the Jacob cycle, Jacob leaving home is a
device to link originally separate central and north-east Palestinian
traditions. Of course, the propriety of making comparisons between ancient Hebrew traditions and comparatively modern
Russian folktales will need to be examined. It may well turn out
to be the case that while comparison of customs and beliefs as
between societies widely separated by time will be fraught with
dangers, it will be difficult to explain away deep structural com-
ponents exhibited in common in tales from widely differing times
and parts of the world. This will hold even if it is acknowledged
that there will be no satisfactory explanation for *why* so many tales
have the apparent common plan structure.

The researches of the classicists and folklorists M. Parry and
A. B. Lord, especially their work on performance and composition,
and on the recurring and standard formulae out of which per-
formers build their oral compositions, have also received attention
from Old Testament scholars.[4] However, a very important book
by an expert on oral traditions and literature has recently suggested
the need for caution in many matters that are commonly taken for
granted. The burden of Ruth Finnegan's *Oral Poetry*,[5] is that
some issues in the study of oral traditions have been over-
simplified.

Interestingly for the present book, and its argument in Chapter
1, Dr. Finnegan shows how the study of oral tradition has been
adversely affected by theories about the nature and development
of societies, over the past two hundred years. She criticizes
assumptions such as that oral transmission is primarily to be
found in 'primitive' societies, or that it is possible to deduce
certain types of society from types of literature, for example, an
'heroic age' from heroic epics. She also shows how complex are
the interrelations between oral and written traditions, and between
performance, composition, transmission, and publication. Although Dr. Finnegan touches only very briefly on oral trans-

---

[4] See the 5th issue of *Semeia*, Montana, Missoula, 1976.
[5] Ruth Finnegan, *Oral Poetry. Its Nature, Significance and Social
Context*, Cambridge, 1977.

mission in ancient societies, her book is one which ought to receive the closest attention from Old Testament scholars.

Jack Goody's *The Domestication of the Savage Mind*[6] is important in relation to the chapter in the present book on primitive mentality, and it also overlaps with Ruth Finnegan's book by exploring the conceptual implications of the introduction of writing into oral communities. Professor Goody argues that to divide societies into primitive and advanced, pre-scientific and scientific, or pre-logical and logical is to bar the way to understanding the real differences between societies, and how it is that human thought has developed. Goody's approach is via the facts of writing and literacy, which, in his view, create a new technology of communication. Writing enables knowledge to be extracted from the social contexts with which it is inextricably bound up in 'oral' societies and situations. Because of it, traditions can be compared side by side, enabling critical faculties to be developed. In 'list science,' the business of classifying items causes reflection on categories, and brings awareness of logical inconsistencies.

Goody states that 'it would be a fundamental error ... to imagine any human society without its quota of what one may legitimately call creative intellectual activity, and even creative intellectuals.'[7] Nevertheless, 'new potentialities for human cognition' are created 'by changes in the means of communication.'[8] Among the material discussed by Goody are the Sumerian examples of 'list science' and the Egyptian Onomastica. The examination of these materials raises the questions as to the relation between written and oral situations, and between literate and illiterate members of a society. A conclusion of interest to Old Testament study is the following about proverbs:

> The influence of writing manifests itself even upon such thoroughly 'folk' material as proverbs, those encapsulations of popular wisdom. One of the favourite subjects for scholars wishing to write down a language for the first time is folk literature, proverbs especially. The effects, particularly upon utterance-embedded forms, is interesting. For by taking the proverb out of the context of speech, by listing it along with a

[6] J. Goody, *The Domestication of the Savage Mind*, Cambridge, 1977.
[7] Op. cit., p. 35.   [8] Op. cit., p. 17.

lot of other similar pithy sentences, one changes the character of the oral form. For example, it then becomes possible to set one proverb against another in order to see if the meaning of one contradicts the meaning of another; they are now tested for a universal truth value, whereas their applicability had been essentially contextual (though phrased in a universal manner).[9]

What is noteworthy about this quotation is that it entirely contradicts the use made by von Rad of proverbs in his *Old Testament Theology*.[10] Von Rad argues that where, in the book of Proverbs, two apparently contradictory proverbs stand side by side, this is evidence for what he calls 'empiric gnomic' thought. The apparent contradictions of Proverbs 26:4–5

> Answer not a fool according to his folly,
> Lest thou be also like unto him.
> Answer a fool according to his folly,
> Lest he be wise in his own conceit.

do not invite us to see a mutually enriching combination of insights based upon the juxtaposition of the sayings. According to von Rad, it is simply that the thought passes from one area of interest to another without any concern for co-ordination. Perhaps it is not without significance that von Rad's interpretation of these proverbs is based upon a theory about an alleged way of thinking characteristic of proverbs, which von Rad takes over from Jolles's *Einfache Formen*.[11] Careful study of Goody's thesis may well result in a re-appraisal of the implications of the so-called Wisdom Literature, and may provide a new way in to the attempt to understand in what ways (if any) ancient Israelite thought differed fundamentally from modern thought.

The books by Ruth Finnegan and Goody raise fundamental questions, and encourage the present author to feel that many of the issues that he has raised in this book are along the right lines, even if the book often seems to be negative in suggesting ways forward. It remains to mention books which will not raise such

[9] Op. cit., pp. 125–6.
[10] G. von Rad, *Theologie des Alten Testaments*, I, pp. 433 ff. E. T. *Old Testament Theology*, Vol. I, pp. 422–3.
[11] See von Rad long quotation from Jolles, pp. 155 f. at p. 435, n. 16; E.T., p. 422, n. 16.

far-reaching questions, but which show that the interest shown by social anthropologists in the Old Testament is a continuing one. Professor Mary Douglas has extended her approaches begun in *Purity and Danger*, especially in two essays 'Deciphering a Meal' and 'Self-Evidence' published in *Implicit Meanings*.[12] As over against some of the writers mentioned in chapter 3 above, who argue that for the Israelites the natural world was alive with evidence of the divine, Douglas regards the natural world as a code with implicit meanings. These implicit meanings did not, in the first instance directly mediate the divine, but helped to suggest a social patterning upon nature, which marked off reality into various spheres of importance, and in this way helped the people to discover and maintain a proper relation with the divine.[13]

The importance of marking off reality into sections is also emphasized in an interesting interpretation of aspects of Old Testament sacrifice in Edmund Leach's *Culture and Communication*.[14] Leach's contribution is very similar to that of Douglas Davies,[15] and emphasizes the value of a sociological interpretation of ritual as a complement to the psychological approaches which have characterized Old Testament study. Leach's statement that he hopes to have shown how, 'in the analysis of ethnography, attention to small details really matters' will, however, produce a smile among Old Testament scholars, in the light of J. A. Emerton's articles on Leach's handling of Genesis 38, where Emerton points out numerous small details which Leach appears to have over-looked.[16] But at least this last point indicates that there is now beginning some sort of new dialogue between Old Testament experts and anthropologists. It is very much to be hoped that it will be a growing dialogue, and one in which both sides seek to learn from the other.

[12] Mary Douglas, *Implicit Meanings. Essays in Anthropology*, London, 1975.
[13] See further my article 'The Old Testament View of Nature: Some Preliminary Questions' in *Instruction and Interpretation (OTS XX)*, Leiden, 1977.
[14] E. R. Leach, *Culture and Communication: The Logic by which Symbols are Connected*, Cambridge, 1976.
[15] See above, p. 114.
[16] Leach, p. 92. Cp. J. A. Emerton, 'An Examination of a Recent Structuralist Interpretation of Genesis XXXVIII' in *V.T.*, Vol. XXVI, pp. 79–98.

Suggested reading

Chapter 1

John Beattie, *Other Cultures*, London (Routledge paperback), 1966.
E. E. Evans-Pritchard, *Essays in Social Anthropology*, London (Faber paperback), 1969.
E. E. Evans-Pritchard, *Social Anthropology*, London, 1951.
E. E. Evans-Pritchard, *Theories of Primitive Religion*, Oxford, 1965.
Godfrey Lienhardt, *Social Anthropology*, London (Oxford paperbacks), 1966 (2nd ed.).
John Rex, *Key Problems of Sociological Theory*, London (Routledge paperback), 1970.

A recent book about what has been described in Chapter 1 as the third period in anthropology is Adam Kuper, *Anthropologists and Anthropology. The British School 1922 1972*, London, 1973. The reader is warned that reviews of this book by anthropologists have tended to be critical; but it will be of interest to Old Testament students, containing as it does, sections on Radcliffe-Brown and Malinowski, and showing how recent anthropology in Britain has gone beyond functionalism.

Readers are also referred to the issue of the *Times Literary Supplement* for 6 July 1973, which contains articles on 'The State of Anthropology.'

Chapter 2

Ruth Benedict, *Patterns of Culture*, London, 1935.
R. M. Dorson, *The British Folklorists*, London, 1968 (see index under 'Doctrine of Survivals').
Mary Douglas, *Purity and Danger*, London, 1966, Ch. 1.
J. J. Honigman (ed.), *Handbook of Social and Cultural Anthropology*, Chicago, 1973, Chs. 2, 3, 4, 8.

Chapter 3

Mary Douglas, *Purity and Danger*, Ch. 5, 'Primitive Worlds,' pp. 73 ff.
S. Diamond (ed.), *Primitive Views of the World*, New York, 1964 (paperback).
E. E. Evans-Pritchard, *Theories of Primitive Religion*.
J. Goody, *The Domestication of the Savage Mind*, Cambridge, 1977.
P. Radin, *Primitive Man as Philosopher*, New York, 1957, (Rev. Ed.).
R. Horton and Ruth Finnegan (eds.), *Modes of Thought*, London, 1973.

Chapter 4

H. M. and N. K. Chadwick, *The Growth of Literature*, 3 vols., Cambridge, 1932–40 (reprinted 1968).
R. M. Dorson, *American Folklore and The Historian*, Chicago, 1971.
Ruth Finnegan, *Oral Poetry. Its Nature, Significance and Social Context*, Cambridge, 1977.
W. D. Hand (ed.), *American Folk Legend*, Berkeley, Calif., 1971.

Chapter 5

R. Fox, *Kinship and Marriage*, Harmondsworth, 1967.
E. E. Evans-Pritchard, *The Nuer*, Oxford, 1940.
June Helm (ed.), *Essays on the Problem of Tribe*, Washington, 1968.
E. R. Leach, *Political Systems of Highland Burma*, London, 1970.

Chapter 6

E. R. Leach, *Genesis as Myth, and Other Essays*, London, 1970.
— *Lévi-Strauss*, London, 1970.
J. Piaget, *Structuralism*, London, 1971.
D. Robey (ed.), *Structuralism: an Introduction*, Oxford, 1973.

Index of Old Testament Passages

Index of Old Testament Names

Index of Authors and Subjects